KU-601-452

DUBLIN

Donated to

**Visual Art Degree
Sherkin Island**

DIT LIBRARY
MOUNTJOY SQUARE

NEW DOMESTIC INTERIORS

Edition 2005

Author: Carles Broto
Publisher: Arian Mostaedi
Editorial Coordinator: Jacobo Krauel
Architectural Advisor: Pilar Chueca
Graphic designer & production: Pilar Chueca, Marta Rojals
Text: contributed by the architects, edited by Amber Ocksassa
English Translation: Amber Ocksassa

Cover photograph: Hiroyuki Hirai

© Carles Broto i Comerma
Jonqueres, 10, 1-5
08003 Barcelona, Spain
Tel.: +34 93 301 21 99
 Fax: +34-93-301 00 21
E-mail: info@linksbooks.net
www. linksbooks.net

All rights reserved. No part of this book may be used or reproduced in any manner whatsoever without written permission except in the case of brief quotations embodied in critical articles and reviews.

Printed in China

new domestic interiors

61227334x

structure

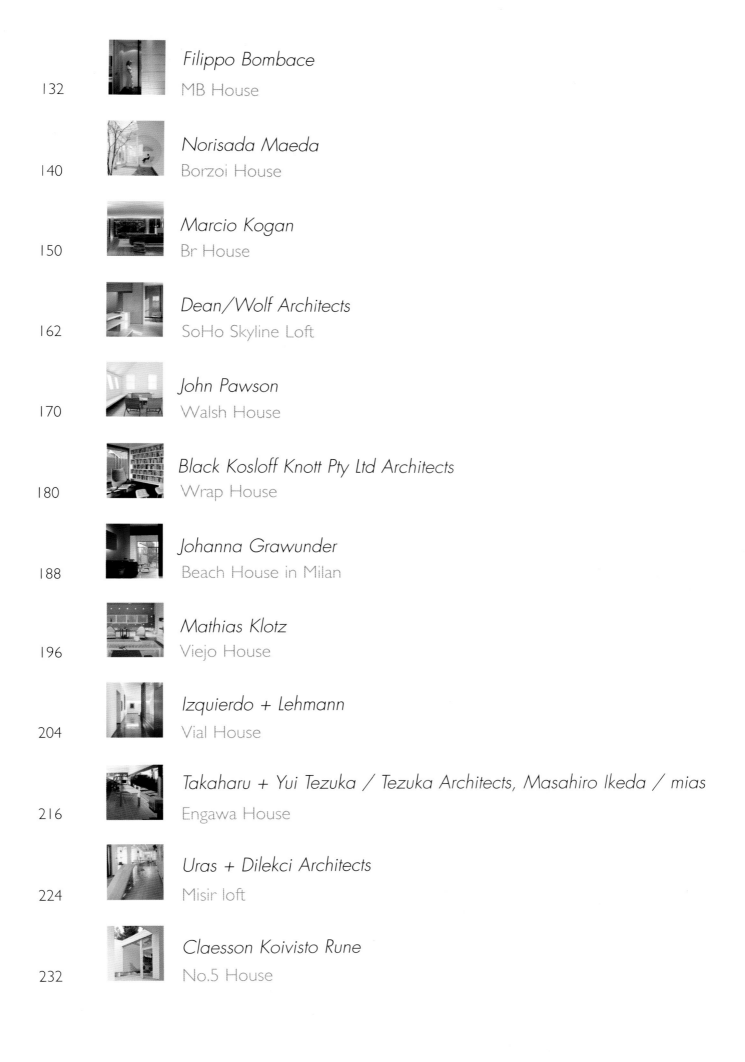

INTRODUCTION

The dwelling is the warm and pleasant refuge in which we feel protected, our place of rest and work, the scenario in which our daily life is enacted, the space in which the essence of each biography is best revealed, a place of encounter and confrontation in which we spend most of our time.

Interior design is currently one of the most innovative disciplines of architecture. Contemporary architects are aware that there is a need for multi-functional and polyvalent spaces and at the same time highly defined spaces that are pleasant and calm and make their inhabitants feel comfortable. They attempt to meet the needs of the 21st century through the interplay of interior and exterior and the integration with the surroundings. Two basic elements in their work are the combination of materials such as wood, glass and steel, and the bold use of open spaces with hardly any divisions, in which light becomes a basic element of the deign.

The search for bold and completely original forms that are adapted to the lifestyle of their inhabitants is often another factor that leads to experimentation and creativity with forms and materials.

This volume presents a wide range of proposals and styles that show the tendencies and ideas of a new interior architecture in which there seems to be no place for unnecessary decorative concessions, and the challenge focuses on creating a space as a sanctuary in which to take refuge from chaos.

In the works of famous and emerging architects such as John Pawson, Mathias Klotz, Shigeru Ban, Delugan Meissl o Claesson Koivisto Rune, we find stimulating answers, ingenious solutions, unexpected points of view and proposals which will certainly influence the concept of architectural interiors.

Shigeru Ban

Naked House

Kawagoe, Japan

Photographs: Hiroyuki Hirai

An unusual client commission requested a home that would "provide the minimum amount of intimacy, so that the members of the family are not isolated from each other - a home that would give each one the freedom to carry out individual activities in a shared atmosphere within the bosom of a close-knit family". The result is a roomy double-height space with uninterrupted sight lines from end to end. Instead of dividing walls demarcating individual bedrooms, the "private" spaces are open volumes equipped with wheels to give them mobility within this hangar-like space. The interior layout can be changed every day if desired; larger "rooms" can be instantly created by removing and stacking their sliding doors. Being lightweight, these volumes can also be wheeled outside in order to make full use of the available space. They can also be used as "bunks", with plenty of sturdy flat space above where kids can play or where objects can be stowed.

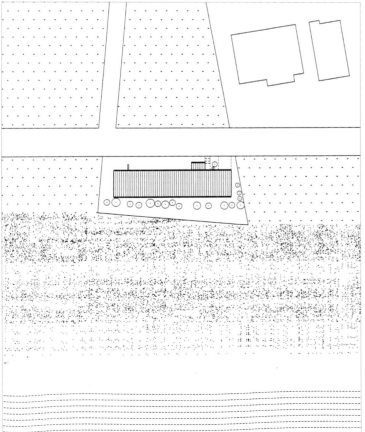

With its hangar-like outward aspect, the home is composed of a single open floor enclosed by translucent walls, which provide uniform lighting throughout the entire space.

33333011530496/747.883

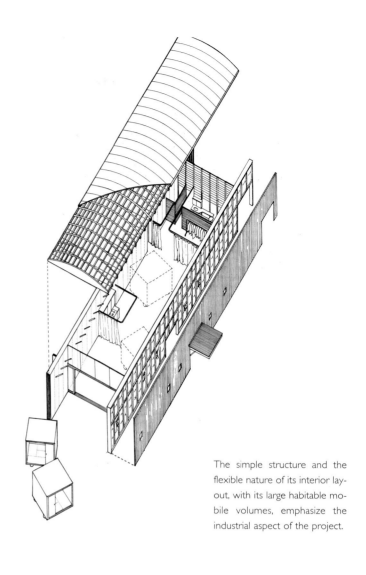

The simple structure and the flexible nature of its interior layout, with its large habitable mobile volumes, emphasize the industrial aspect of the project.

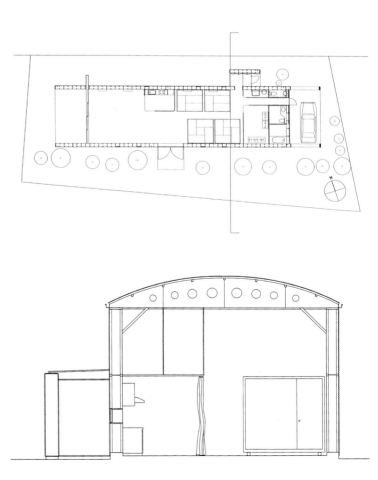

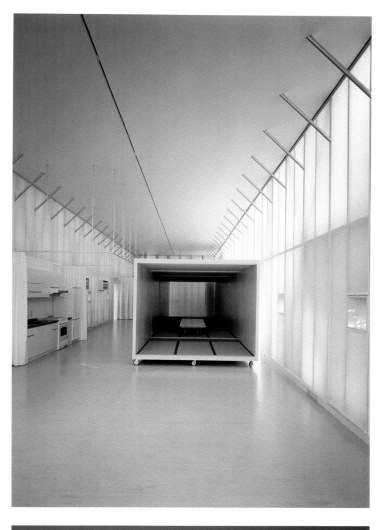

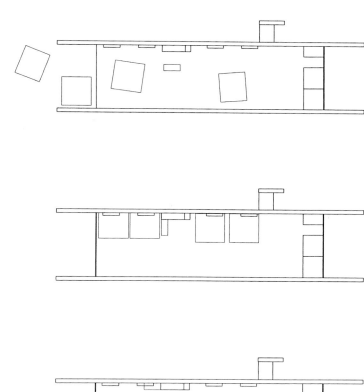

Layout variations

Carlos Zapata, Wood + Zapata

Private House

Quito, Ecuador

Photographs: Undine Pröhl

Located on a spectacular site minutes outside of Quito, this private house has just been completed. The 8000-square-foot main house features four bedrooms, six bathrooms, kitchen, dining room, living room, playroom, family room and an artist's studio adjacent to the master bedroom.

A profusion of unexpected geometries greets the inhabitants at every turn - there is scarcely a right angle in the entire design, with entirely glazed walls tilting outward, angled doorways and gentle curves coming together in one unified whole. The warmth of wood contrasts with the home's extensive glazed surfaces.

One of the most unusual features of the house is the lap pool that begins inside the house and continues outside to cantilever over the cliff. The walkway alongside the pool cantilevers out even further, offering a sweeping view of the Andes Mountains sitting opposite the site.

The structure of the building is primarily of reinforced concrete and has been designed to withstand earthquakes.

Much of the artwork showcased in the house is the work of the owner's father, Oswaldo Viteri, who is one of the most recognized artists in Ecuador.

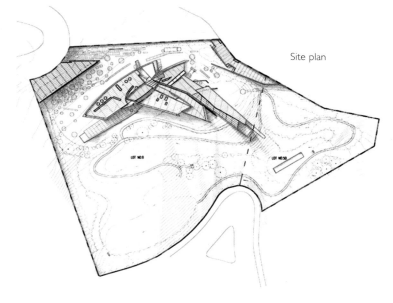

Site plan

The curved wall of the east faced has been designed to isolate the home from its built surroundings. There, the anti-seismic reinforced concrete structure has been left unfinished on the lower level and clad in metal on the upper part to camouflage the only two windows.

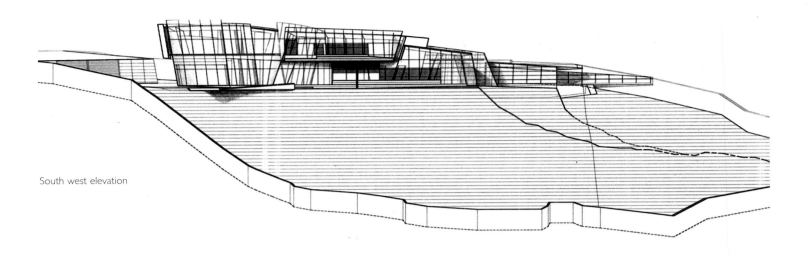

South west elevation

The layout of the house is almost traditional, with public functions and a separate service area on the ground floor and the private area upstairs. The main stairs feature a curved surface that is reflected on the first floor in the volume of the master bedroom.

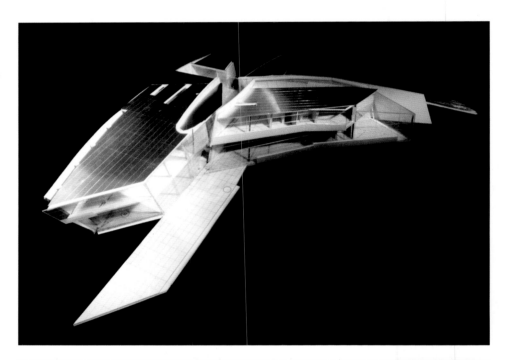

North east elevation

North west elevation

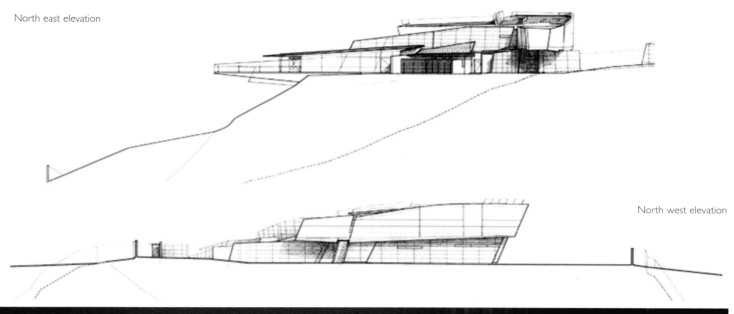

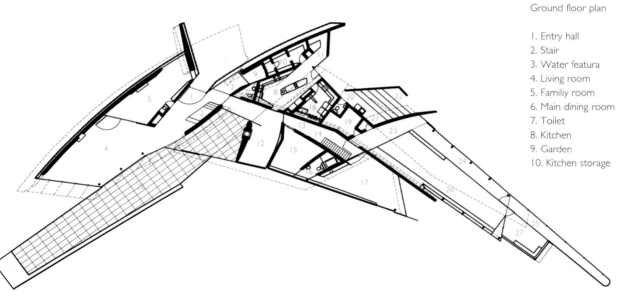

Ground floor plan

1. Entry hall	11. Kitchen dining area
2. Stair	12. Dining room
3. Water featura	13. Rear hall
4. Living room	14. Stair
5. Familiy room	15. Guest bedroom
6. Main dining room	16. Guest bathroom
7. Toilet	17. Playroom
8. Kitchen	18. Laundry room
9. Garden	19. Storage
10. Kitchen storage	20. Toilet
	21. Storage
	22. Laundry drying area
	23. Pool area
	24. Indoor deck
	25. Outdoor deck
	26. Lap pool
	27. Wading pool
	28. Dining terrace

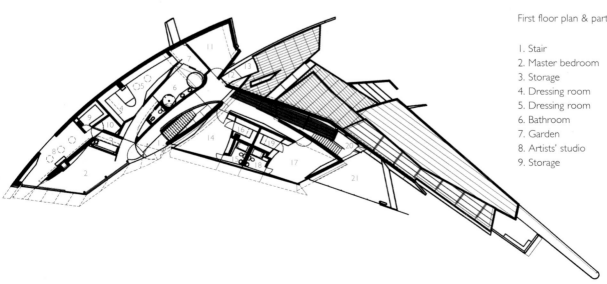

First floor plan & partial roof plans

1. Stair	10. Safe room
2. Master bedroom	11. Exercise room
3. Storage	12. Glass sloping to
4. Dressing room	below
5. Dressing room	13. Open to below
6. Bathroom	14. Children's bedroom
7. Garden	15. Bathroom
8. Artists' studio	16. Closet
9. Storage	17. Children's bedroom
	18. Bathroom
	19. Closet
	20. Hall
	21. Open to playroom

With natural light and wide-open views being the dominant themes in the design of the house, the interior displays a minimal palette of materials, with unfinished concrete, maple and cherry wood and slabs of limestone providing warmth and style.

SCDA Architects Pte. Ltd.

Andrew Road House

Singapore

Photographs: Albert Lim K. S.

The house consists of three flat-roofed rectangular blocks on a rectangular site that slopes approximately four meters from east to west. The three blocks are, respectively, a long timber-clad volume, a similar unit enveloped in a light metal screen and a third block in the form of an open-sided pavilion. All have flat roofs of zinc titanium.

Immediately evident is SCDA's strategy of choreographing a route in a series of staccato movements. The first block that one encounters is the single-story reception pavilion that is open on all four sides. This transparent space is revealed upon passing through an opening in a stone wall, which is located transversely across the pedestrian entrance axis. Beyond the reception pavilion is the swimming pool.

Having arrived at the 'center' one turns abruptly to the right and encounters the largest of the three blocks, containing the principal living and dining areas, the master bedroom and the secondary bedrooms. On plan this is a timber-clad rectangular structure that runs parallel to the northern boundary of the site and it is visually dominant in the overall composition.

Returning to the entrance pavilion; located at the southern end is a three-meter-high circular "lantern" constructed of timber, lined internally with a woven steel fabric. This lantern is lit from within and is the visual focus of the pavilion.

The third block is located in the south-east corner of the site overlooking the swimming pool and a waterfall. This is the lowest area of the site so that, although two-stories high, its roof is at the same level as the single story entrance pavilion. Again the architecture unfolds as a series of carefully orchestrated phenomenological experiences.

A sub basement entrance court with parking for four cars is located beneath the entrance pavilion.

The largest of the blocks is a timber-clad volume containing the principal living and dining areas, the master bedroom and the secondary bedrooms. It is entered by crossing a bridge and passing a thick screen wall so that the experience of the interior is delayed.

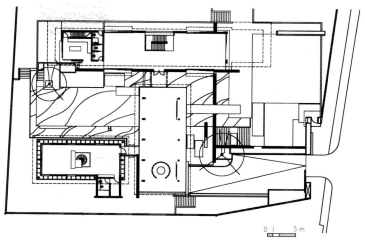

The volume abutting the swimming pool (seen below) is set perpendicular to the entirely glazed entrance pavilion. Although its roof is level with the single-story volume of the entrance pavilion, it is a two-story volume that sits on the lowest part of the site. It is clad in a permeable metal screen.

Michele Bonino, Subhash Mukerjee, Federica Patti & Martina Tabò

"One meter above", House in Torino

Turin, Italy

Photographs: Beppe Giardino

A couple in their thirties bought an elegant corner apartment in a 19th century building in the center of Turin.

The apartment was very spacious and had interesting views towards a large gardened boulevard.

The main problem of the remodeling that Coex were asked to design was the big, dark entrance: the clients loved its finely worked continuous terrazzo floor and of course wanted to make it a pleasing and functional space. On the other hand it had no windows and received no natural light. Coex decided to make that space the core and engine of the whole flat. The entrance is invaded by a massive volume containing "dark functions" - a shower and some storage space. To preserve the integrity of the floor, the volume "flies" one meter above and the contained functions are only accessible from the back. The volume also serves as a big lamp for the entrance providing direct illumination throughout this level. To take advantage of the views and to enhance the apartment's sense of spaciousness, the two requested bathrooms are compressed behind the volume.

In accordance with the clients' brief, the other rooms have been left almost undesigned, thus emphasizing the contrast between the dark and dense private areas and the light-filled, airy living spaces.

Central to the design is this masonry volume cantilevered out over the entrance and containing the main bedroom's walk-in closet and an open cloakroom in one corner. Here, the existing terrazzo floor has been preserved in its entirety.

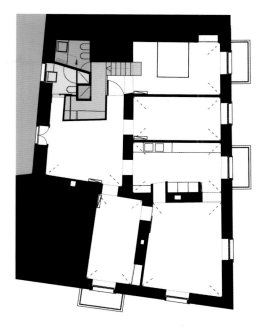

The kitchen is well-communicated with the living/dining area, although visually separated by a fixed unit housing kitchen equipment and appliances. All of the flooring in this area is the apartment's original oak parquet.

The stairs to the bathroom are paved in dark Brazilian ferrous slate, with the warm beech plywood flooring of the master bedroom set in gentle counterpoint.

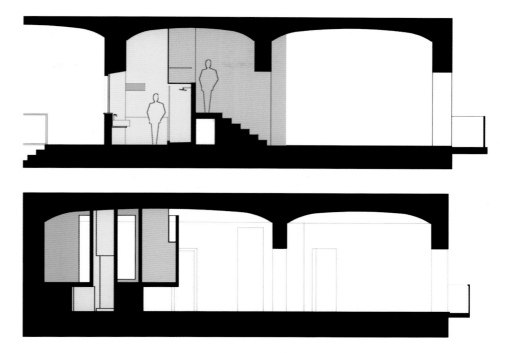

The raised bathroom and walk-in closet sit adjacent to the master bedroom. This volume, which sits one meter above the rest of the apartment in the corner of the plan, is an ingenious reworking of limited space.

Mark Cigolle & Kim Coleman

TR-I House and Studio

California, USA

Photographs: Undine Pröhl

This house and studio, designed by two architects for themselves, their two children, and their extended family, is conceived as a laboratory to test ideas about light, space, and material. The sloping site is located a few blocks from the ocean and has views of the coastline and Santa Monica Bay to the east and the Santa Monica Mountains to the north. The elements of the project are divided into two typologies: habitable walls that define the site, and volumes that define hierarchically-important spaces.

Two-story lichen-colored rough cement plaster walls, linked by poured-in-situ concrete walls and stairs defining a walled courtyard, form an L that bounds the site on two sides, providing privacy from and screening views of adjacent properties. These walls establish a bounded space for family activities and an armature for the series of one-story smooth plaster and metal volumes. The interlocking volumes establish a dialogue between a collection of elements with distinct qualities: solid or void, light or heavy, open or closed, rooted to the ground or additive.

The kitchen, dining room, and den occupy a void below a second story sheathed in corrugated copper. The living room has two views, one an internal view to the walled entry court, and the other extending across the swimming pool to the mountains beyond. The form of the solar-heated pool is absorbed into the organization of the house, consolidating the treatment of building and landscape. The angled cement-colored smooth plaster walls of the living room screen the interior of the room from the driveway and street. A skylight supported by exposed joists over the stair brings light into the center of the house. In contrast, concrete walls and polished or washed sand concrete floors anchor the house to the ground and provide a sense of ambiguity and extension between inside and outside.

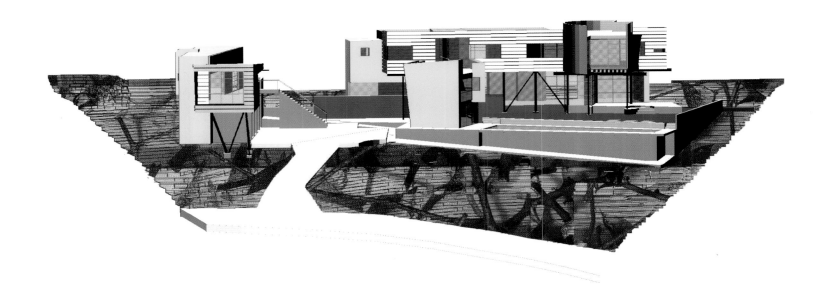

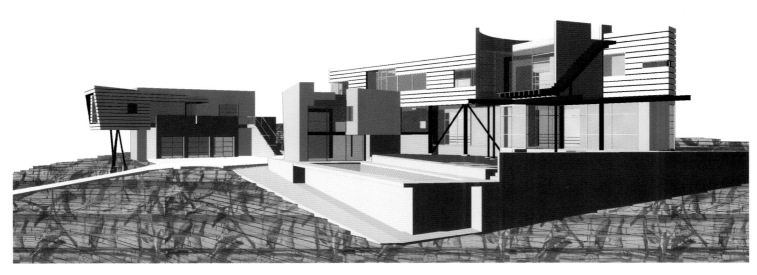

The colors of the materials are echoed in the vegetation: red-barked eucalyptus trees, red fountain grass, chartreuse licorice plant and zebra grass, gray-barked sycamore and olive trees. On the deck above the living room, potted citrus trees provide fruit and fragrant blossoms, while the private roof deck above the master bedroom offers a panoramic view.

Two-story lichen-colored rough cement plaster walls, linked by poured-in-situ concrete walls and stairs defining an enclosed court-yard, form an L that bounds the site on two sides, providing privacy from adjacent properties. Welded and braced steel moment frames allow for an open plan and large areas of glass on the first floor.

Upper floor plan

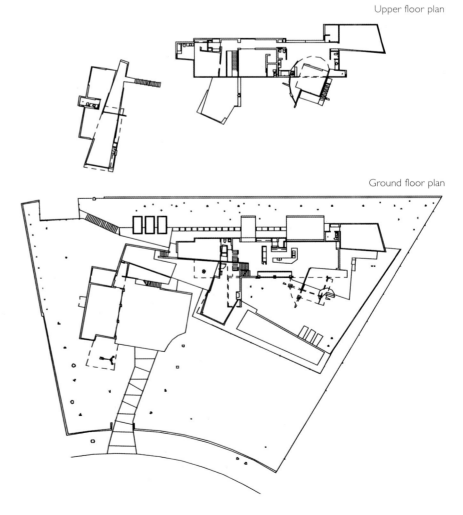

Ground floor plan

As in the copper-clad studio, the zinc-lined master bedroom has floor-to-ceiling glass doors framing extensive views of the ocean. The house relies on natural ventilation augmented by radiant heat embedded in the floors. Transparent and white glass allows sunlight into the interior from all sides.

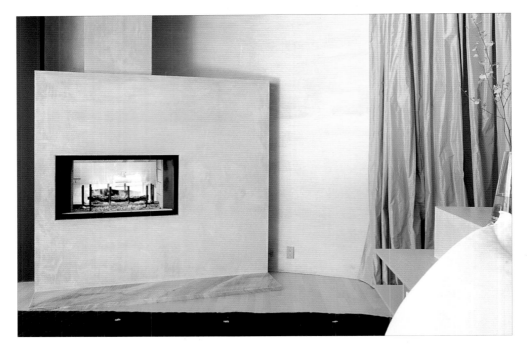

Adrià+Broid+Rojkind

Casa F2

Ciudad de Mexico, Mexico

Photographs: Undine Pröhl

This single-family home is set on the outskirts of the metropolitan area of Mexico City. An "L" scheme has been adapted to a triangular plot while capturing the best views and avoiding those of the neighboring houses. A circulation axis provides the schematic structure of the house, from the entrance to the linear stairway that joins the three floors, which are located in a single wing of the home. A concrete "box" with perforations is set flush between the two lightweight slabs of the perpendicular body, its opacity and solidity contrasting with the transparency and lightness of the planes that make up the house. The house is set along the slope of the terrain, thus making it only necessary to reinforce the overhang of certain concrete elements in order to ensure sufficient shade in the summer and the passage of sunlight in the winter. The clients, a young couple planning on having children, wanted a house that would be open enough to be able to enjoy its integration in the surrounding natural landscape, but without sacrificing intimacy. A TV and movie room were added to the entrance/service areas and living/dining room, which are all located on the access level. The bedrooms are on the upper floor, while the study and library are on the lower.

>From the very first stages of sketching and modeling, a great deal of clarity and straightforwardness in the building process was achieved. This avoidance of ornamentation, with the superposition of finishing materials over the rough foundation, meant that the structural elements should also serve as enclosing elements and the finishes should be both for interior and exterior. The concrete slabs comprising the access level and roof have an inverted slope that enhances its lightweight aspect, thereby emphasizing its streamlined horizontal lines. The area abutting the study and library on the lower floor frees up a flat space with a grassy garden area that is suitable for all kinds of domestic activities and festive occasions. Furthermore, this garden has been set up to visually blend in with the nearby federally protected reserve land. An outdoor jacuzzi is located at one end and, at the back of the house, a patio serves at once as exterior dining area and water mirror. A number of existing trees were left in place in the entrance area, growing out from perforations in the concrete slab and creating a welcoming shade at the home's entryway.

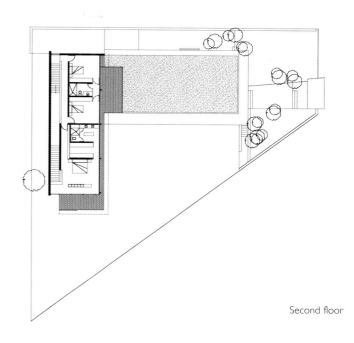

Second floor

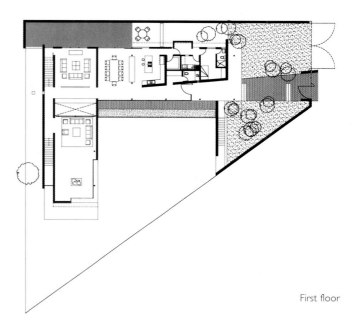

First floor

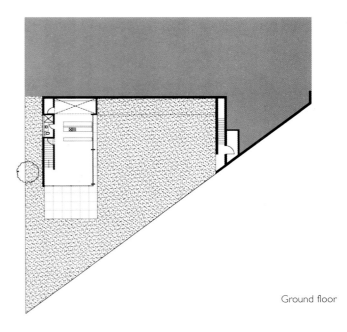

Ground floor

The topography, the views, the orientation of the home and the program were the predominant considerations in the project. The lay of the land enabled the project to be viewed as split-level, comprised of entry section and garden section. The program helped create an L-shaped layout that would separate the uses and functions of the home's different levels, thus adapting it to the particularities of the site.

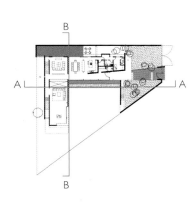

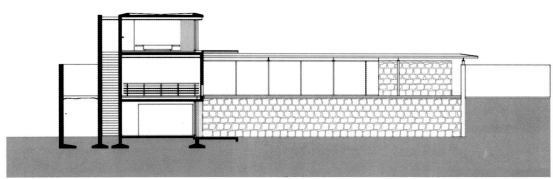

Section AA

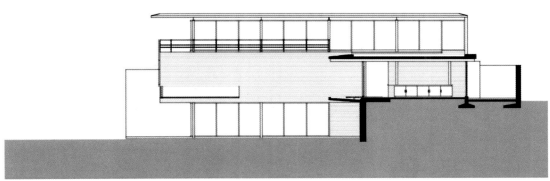

Section BB

Consideration of the views determined both the layout of the home and the placement of its windows and other openings. The south-facing side enjoys choice, untouchable views of federal reserve land; on the other side, attempts have been made to screen views from the neighboring houses, which, from a design perspective, are formally deficient.

The program and building process adhered closely to clear, simple strategies concerning the structural, surface and finishing aspects. Resources such as steel columns to emphasize the apparent weightlessness of the slabs and unfinished concrete walls to define the domestic spaces were used. Special attention was paid to the falsework done in pine stakes, in order to give maximum expression to the interior and exterior surfaces.

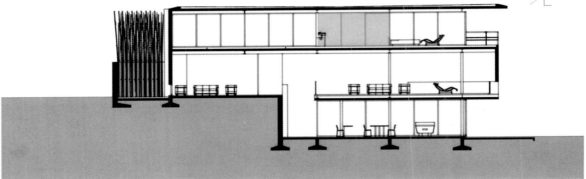

Ángel Sánchez-Cantalejo, Vicente Tomás

House in Santa Margarita

Majorca, Spain

Photographs: Alejo Bagué

The plot for this home is set at the top of a hill next to a church on the outer edge of the urban quarter of the town of Santa Margarita; from here, there are excellent views of the Majorcan beach with the Serra de Tramuntana mountains as a backdrop. A concrete wall generates the entrance to the home and definitively shuts out views of the backyards and patios of the neighboring houses. An opening in this wall provides the entrance to the home through a courtyard. Set adjacent to this main wall are three more structural concrete walls that determine the layout of the ground floor and open outward to views of the beach and the side of the hill. A wood-clad box is set atop these walls; it is closed on the town-facing side yet open to views on the other, thus establishing a dialogue between the solidity of concrete, the lightness of wood and the fragility of glass. The ground floor is laid out along a length-wise axis, which is open on both ends. The bedrooms and their respective bathrooms are set to one side of this axis, while on the other are a double-height space and stairwell, providing vertical communication with the upper floor, and two courtyards. One of these is adjoined to the master bedroom, with the other located at the far end of the axis. Reinforced concrete slabs and walls poured in situ form the basis of the structure. The interior and exterior flooring is wood, as is the interior carpentry. The cladding of the "box" has been done with fillets affixed to the outer walls and two-centimeter-thick wood boards set eight millimeters apart. The fold of the house's main wall generates an exterior living room-like space with 10x12 modules. While the paving of the terraces, which embrace the pool of black slate, are wood, the flooring of the large "exterior living room" is of floating concrete in 1x1 modules. Only a handful of window-like openings visually join this space with the rest of the plot and with the church.

Southwest elevation

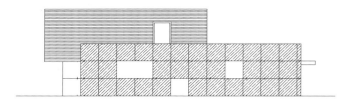

Elevation northeast

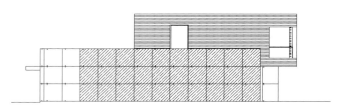

Northeast elevation

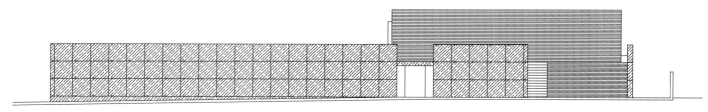

Southeast elevation

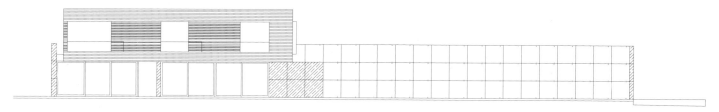

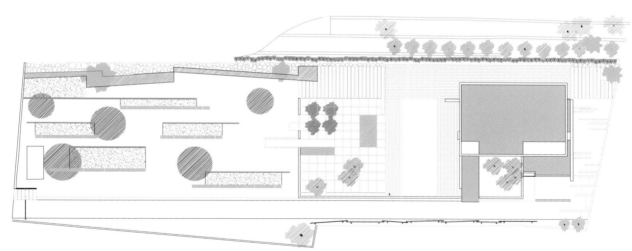

The project is located in the municipality of Santa Margarita on the northeast part of the island of Majorca. The site is set at the top of a hill, next to a church, on the outer edge of the town. Here, there are excellent views of the Majorcan beach, with the Serra de Tramuntana mountains as a backdrop.

Section AA   Section BB

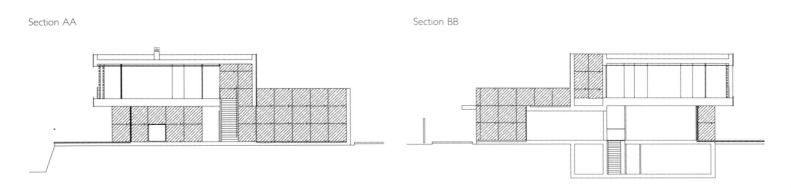

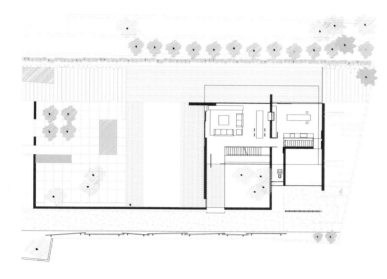

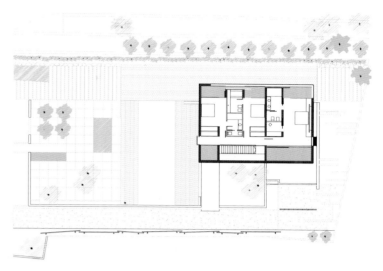

The main program consists of two floors, with the living room, kitchen and garage set on the ground floor while the first floor takes in the bedrooms. All the spaces, both inside and out, have been patterned on a 1.35 square meter base, formed by the metal formwork of the walls and slabs. The amount of materials has been kept to a minimum: concrete, wood and glass make up the dividing walls and cladding.

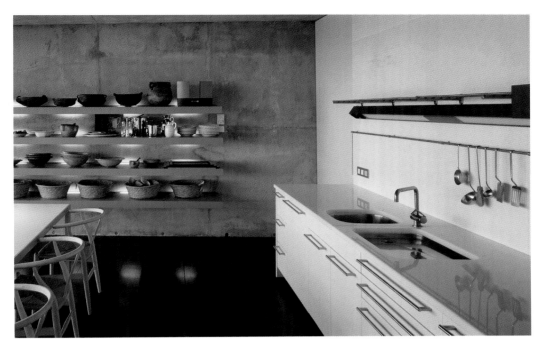

Delugan_Meissl

Ray 1

Vienna, Austria

Photographs: Rupert Steiner

This apartment, situated on the roof of a 1960s office building in the middle of the rooftop landscape of Vienna's fourth district, has evolved from the spatial quality of its location. The design addresses the inevitable strict building regulations for rooftop expansion while not entirely giving in to them, instead employing a re-interpretation of these regulations.

Recesses and folds create transparent zones and sheltered terraced landscapes on both sides of the building, providing the opportunity to experience the structure's open layout from the entrance all the way up to the accessible roof area.

The outer skin, which is coated with Alucobond, defines the contours of the apartment's interior as well, suggesting varying valences for different zones and niches. The intention here was to create a shell that would function as a programmable medium for furniture, or furniture that would be transformed through the architecture.

The spacious living area and the centrally located kitchen are raised almost a meter above the enclosed bedroom zones, giving them an intimate character. The open kitchen unit, located on a plateau of the ramp of the living area, is the transition point between introverted and extroverted zones and acts as the hub of the flow of interior spaces.

The vast, leather-upholstered relaxation zone on the same level as the work area emerges from a section that extends out beyond the property line. Here, the use of glazed surfaces with load-bearing capacity fully meets the demand for a flowing architectonic space whose perimeter signals distinction, permeability, and continuity between interior and exterior. At the far end, the living space becomes wider through a transparent corner of large frameless sliding glass doors. These can be pushed completely out of the way to afford access to a terrace with a sunken basin along its edge. From here one has a seamless and unimpeded view of the city.

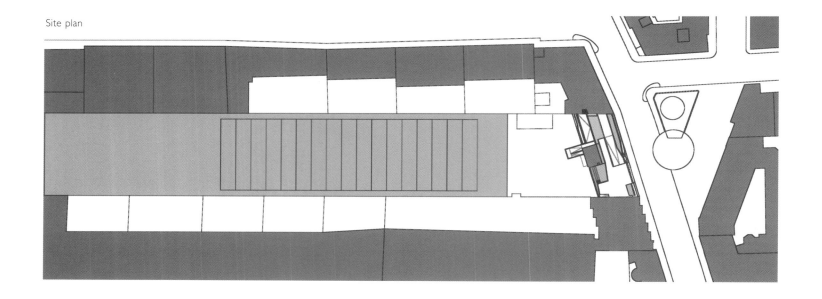

Site plan

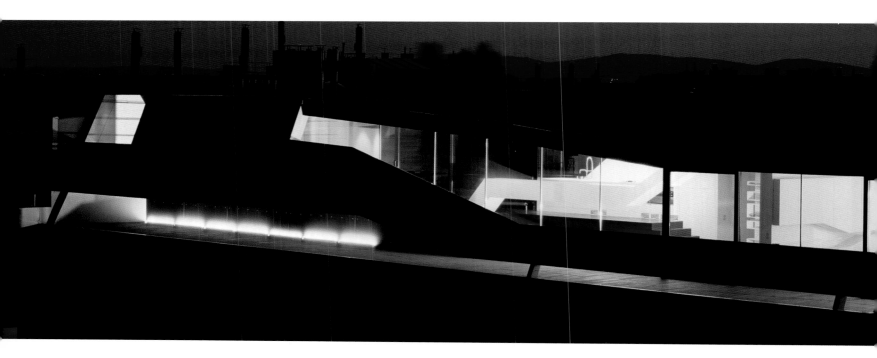

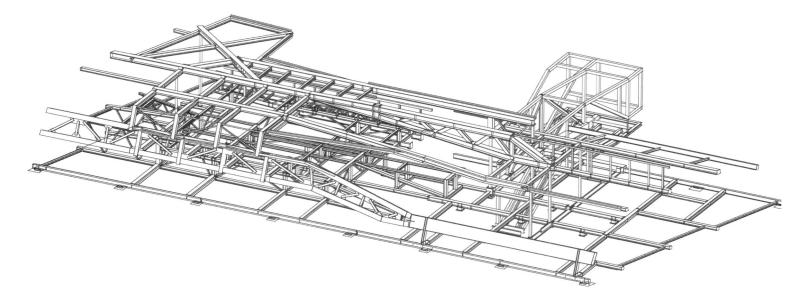

A homogenous steel framework was used to transfer the load evenly over the entire roof surface. The major loads of the roof construction are supported by gables, while the staggered and sloping levels of the rooftop landscape serve to achieve a spatial flow largely unhampered by supports. The interior space is designed as a loft whose various functional areas are defined by different floor levels.

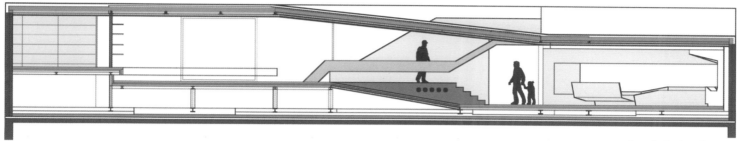

Longitudinal section

Street elevation

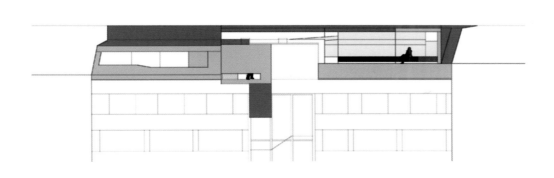

Courtyard elevation

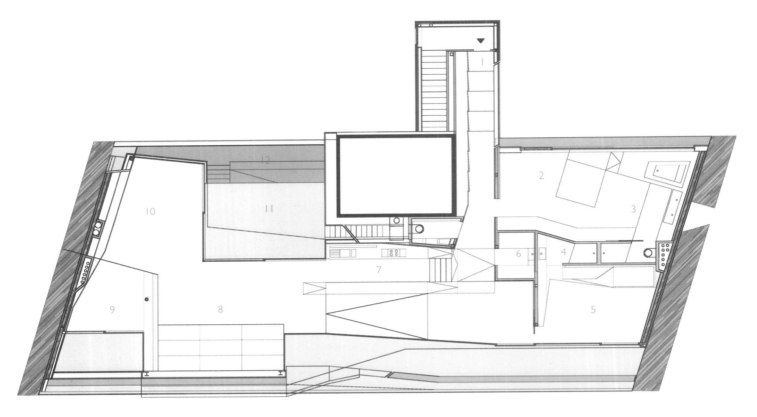

Ground floor plan

1. Entrance
2. Parents' bedroom
3. Bathroom area
4. Bathroom
5. Daughter's bedroom
6. Walk-in closet
7. Kitchen
8. Living area
9. Office
10. Dining area
11. Terrace
12. Pool

Cross sections

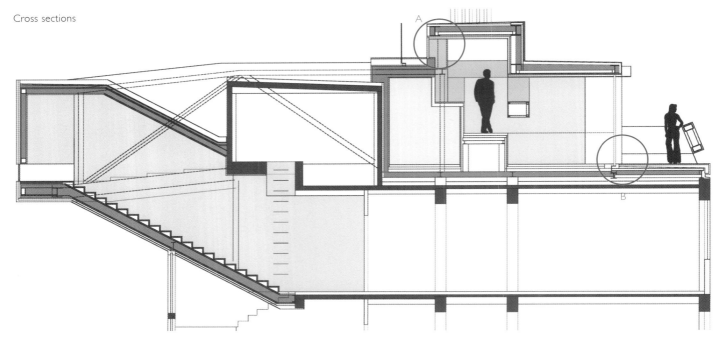

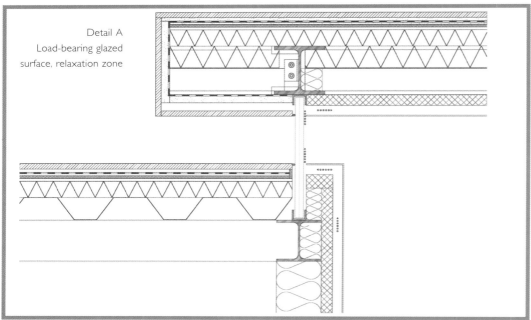

Detail A
Load-bearing glazed
surface, relaxation zone

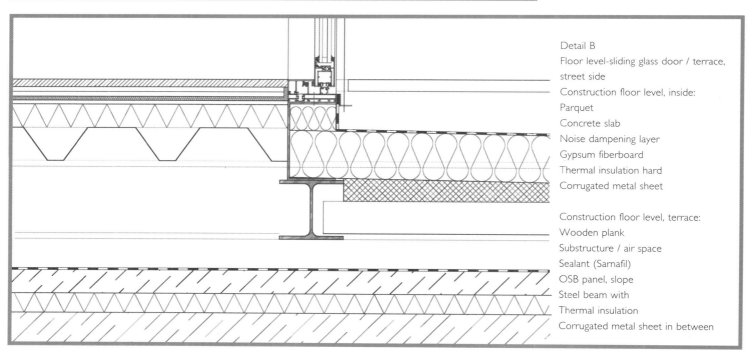

Detail B
Floor level-sliding glass door / terrace,
street side
Construction floor level, inside:
Parquet
Concrete slab
Noise dampening layer
Gypsum fiberboard
Thermal insulation hard
Corrugated metal sheet

Construction floor level, terrace:
Wooden plank
Substructure / air space
Sealant (Sarnafil)
OSB panel, slope
Steel beam with
Thermal insulation
Corrugated metal sheet in between

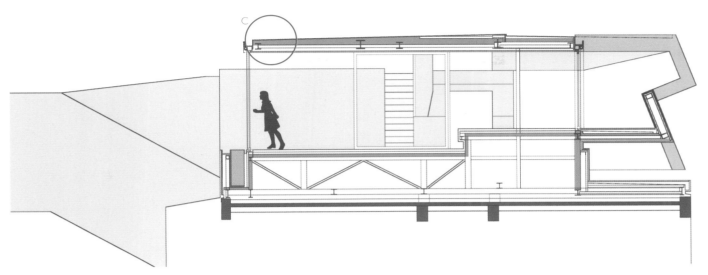

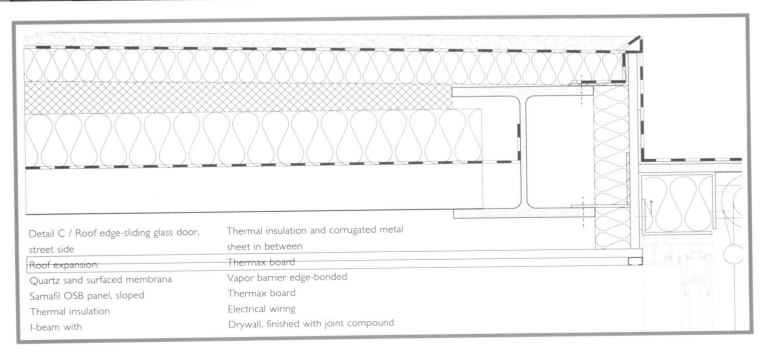

Detail C / Roof edge-sliding glass door,
street side

Roof expansion:

Quartz sand surfaced membrana

Sarnafil OSB panel, sloped

Thermal insulation

I-beam with

Thermal insulation and corrugated metal
sheet in between

Thermax board

Vapor barrier edge-bonded

Thermax board

Electrical wiring

Drywall, finished with joint compound

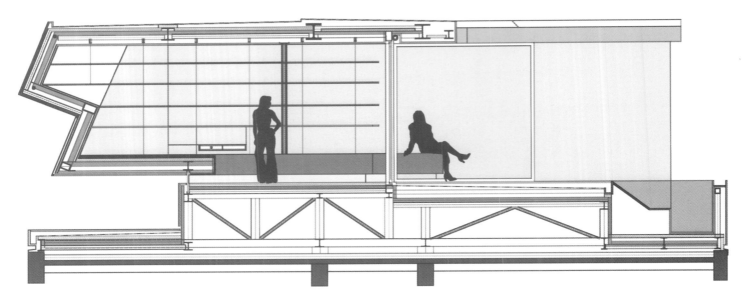

Cross sections

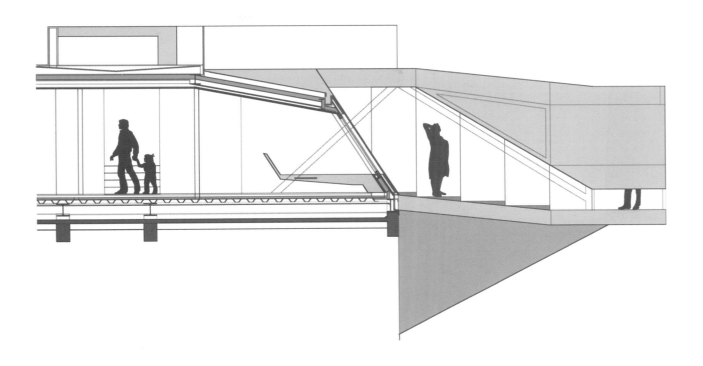

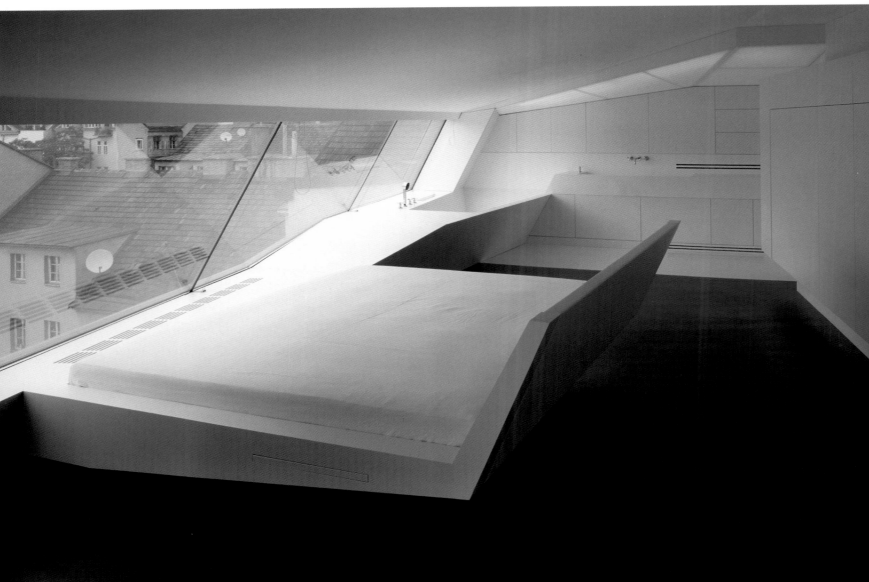

Takaharu + Yui Tezuka / Tezuka Architects,
Masahiro Ikeda / mias

Borzoi House

Katsuura Chiba, Japan

Photographs: Katsuhisa kida

The site is located in a suburban area of Tokyo that was recently developed from farmland into residential lots of approximately one hundred square meters. The neighborhood is characterized by brand-new, two-storey wooden houses which are being built in a variety of colors. Sooner or later the site itself will be surrounded by similar buildings on three sides, but otherwise nothing particular emerges from the context.

If one followed the example of other constructions in the area, a two-storey house built near the northern edge of the lot would leave virtually no space for a garden. On the other hand, a single-storey structure would be dominated by the neighboring houses, and left without much light. Large windows on the southern façade would be no answer either, since curtains would have to be shut at all times to ensure privacy.

The surface of the site is roughly 148.5 meters square. A 60 percent building-to-land ratio would leave nearly 90 square meters for a single-storey house, the equivalent of a two-storey house with 115 square meters. Such a space would provide enough room to accommodate a married couple.

The structure of the House to Catch the Sky III was designed very simply: a square box with a central light well that was created by cutting and lowering a rectangular portion of the roof above the core. The sky is the only direction towards which both a certain privacy and space can be guaranteed in Japanese urban areas. The high-side opening was thus designed to circumscribe the view to the sky and the roofs of surrounding buildings. In this way privacy does not become a matter of concern, and the sunlight can penetrate the house equally throughout the day.

Measuring approximately 150 m², the plot is set on the outskirts of Tokyo in an area that had once been used as farmland, but which has recently become populated with residential plots occupied by new, two-story wooden houses.

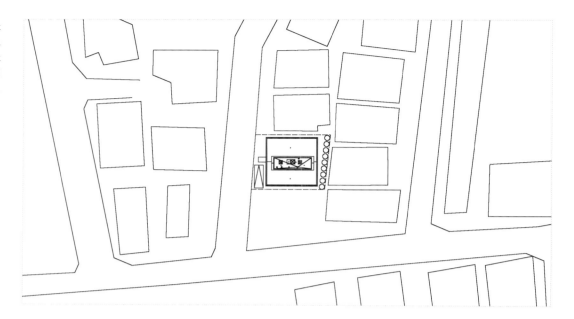

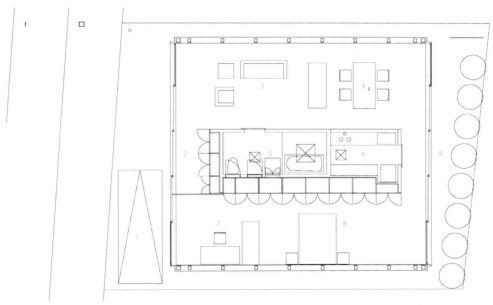

Floor plan

1. Parking
2. Entrance
3. Living room
4. Dining room
5. Bathroom
6. Kitchen
7. Office
8. Bedroom
9. Yard

Longitudinal section

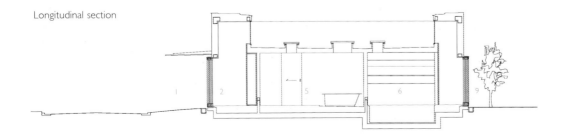

With a flat roof 3.2 meters above ground, the height of the building stands well within regulations. The whole structure is actually one single volume, with a bedroom and a living room occupying two equal spaces on both sides of the core, which contains the water storage systems.

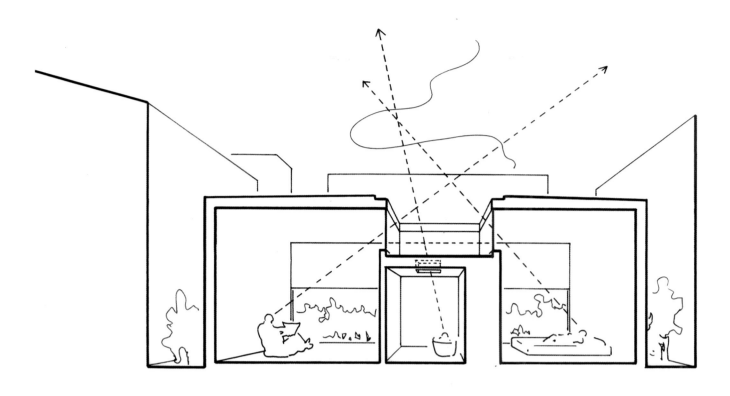

D.I.T.
LIBRARY
MOUNTJOY SQ.

Driendl architects

Solar Deck

Vienna, Austria

Photographs: Contributed by the architects

The 14th district of Vienna is a typical suburban village district. People which live here reached a rather higher living standard and dwell primary in private houses, mostly situated on small and tight sites.

Also the site, which the Viennese clients acquired is small and tight - this makes the neighbour houses appear very close. Exactly that was the architectural challenge, to built under such circumstances a private house with 290m² useable space and a double garage.

Georg Driendl arranged the bedrooms and all adjacent rooms in the ground floor. The living room and the kitchen build together a very spacious level without columns in the upper floor. This floor is additional widened with correlating terraces on the east,- south,- and west side.

Thereby an amazing effect was created: it seems that the living room increases over the terraces and which makes appear that the neighbours moved into wide distance.

The big wall on the north side made of reinforced concrete (like the foundation and basement) saves the heat and reflexes it to the rooms. The upper floor is a self-supporting steel construction in addition with prefabricated wood and glass units. Large-scaled glazing in the upper floor as well a transparent stripe along the north side of the roof enable a pleasant light flooded feeling. The light- strip on the ceiling creates an interesting illumination as well as an excellent thermal situation.

Ground floor and upper floor are connected trough a levitate staircase and a large opened space along the north side wall. So one of the majority aims of the architect "daylight into the smallest corner" was realised.

The site was small and hemmed in, as was the surrounding built environment, making the neighboring homes seem even closer than they were. The challenge was to build a private house with a useable surface area of 290 m² with a two-car garage under these conditions.

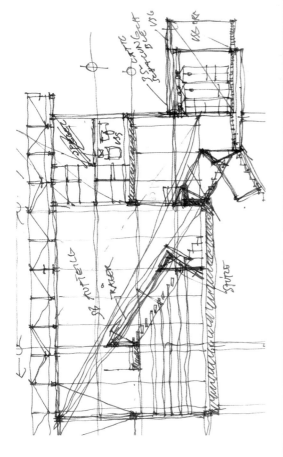

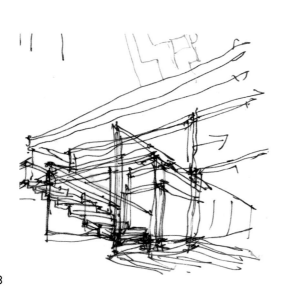

Basement floor plan

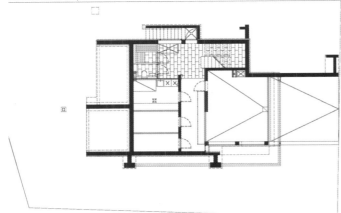

Ground floor plan

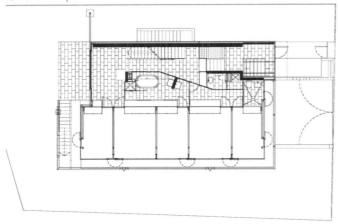

First floor plan

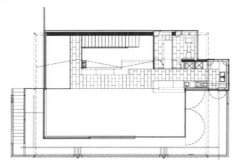

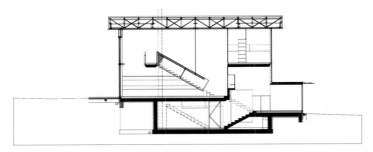

Longitudinal section

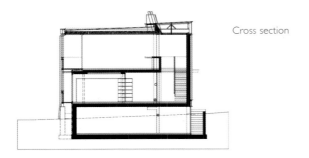

Cross section

The home has been designed to keep energy consumption to a minimum and to make use of sunlight in the interior as much as possible. The structure consists of a concrete base with a steel framework; the roof has been built with lattice girders and the partitions are of prefabricated modules.

Joel Sanders Architect

Millenium Apartment

New York, USA

Photographs: Peter Aaron / ESTO

The Millennium apartment, an 1800-square-foot gut renovation, is a re-thinking of an ordinary but over-determined domestic zone: closets, which, like bathrooms, are typically cordoned off from public view.

The first design decision was to raise the existing walls that divided the space into a series of isolated rooms unsuited to the client's brief: a flexible open plan with a resilient dance floor for ballet practice that also accommodates out-of-town guests and plenty of storage space.

All domestic programs (entry, living/dining area, dance practice, study, master bedroom, and master bath) form a chain of overlapping spaces that flow around the centerpiece of the project - a central service core that contains plumbing (guest bath) and storage (master closet, home entertainment, bookshelves, appliances).

However, if service cores are typically treated as opaque masses that shield their contents from view, in the Millennium the core selectively reveals rather than conceals. Like a lantern, the translucent glass core provides the apartment's principal light source. Silhouettes of backlit bodies and household objects are veiled behind this glowing container.

In an effort to maximize multi-purpose living, every square foot of floor area is designed to assume a variety of functions. When guests arrive, concealed panels unfold to convert the dance practice area into a private guest suite. Similarly, pivoting panels allow the spacious bedroom to be subdivided into a private study or a second guestroom.

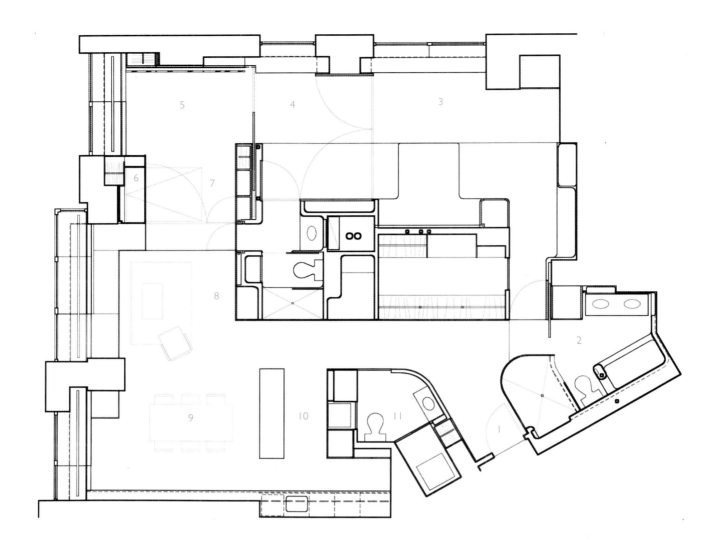

1. Entrance
2. Master bathroom
3. Bedroom
4. Library
5. Dance practice space
6. Foldaway bed
7. Lighted closets
8. Living room
9. Dining room
10. Kitchen
11. Bathroom
12. Dressing room

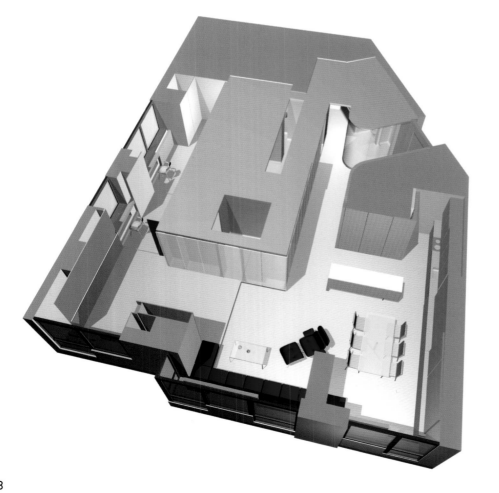

The translucent panels of all service areas have been backlit, selectively revealing their contents while also providing the apartment's principal light source. In maximizing multi-purpose space, concealed panels unfold to convert the dance practice area into a private guest suite. Similarly, pivoting panels allow the spacious bedroom to be subdivided into a private study or a second guestroom.

Atelier Bow Wow

Asama House

Kariuzawa, Japan

Photographs: Atelier Bow Wow

This site is located on the edge of the famous mountain resort Karuizawa, 2 hours by car from Tokyo. Since it borders farm land, the area is a mixture of holiday homes and farm houses. To the west are rice paddies and to the east is forest. The project is a simple, single room for a family and is surrounded by 15-meter-high trees.

All the living spaces directly benefit from the daily shifts of natural light and views of the canopy of trees surrounding the home. The building is square in plan, with a pyramidal roof. The issue for this project was how to affect the purity of this form with the specific nature of the various orientations.

The ceiling space is divided into 5 portions by suspended walls giving a suggestion of rooms. The suspended walls act as large beams so that columns are not required, and a single space can be maintained below.

The position of the suspended walls is determined by the combination of proportions to suit activities such as dining, living, studying, sleeping and washing. The angles of the roof planes are also defined by these proportions. The architects made every effort to incorporate the site's abundant light into the scheme. While the trunk-scape of the forest is framed, the tops of the trees with a backdrop of blue sky are pulled into the space by large openings. By planning the layout in this way, each of the 9 external surfaces of the house obtained an opening. The light qualities entering through each of these openings measure changing time, seasons and orientation. At sunset, a particular portion of the ceiling space becomes stained in a changing hue of orange, while the other portions show various shades of gray.

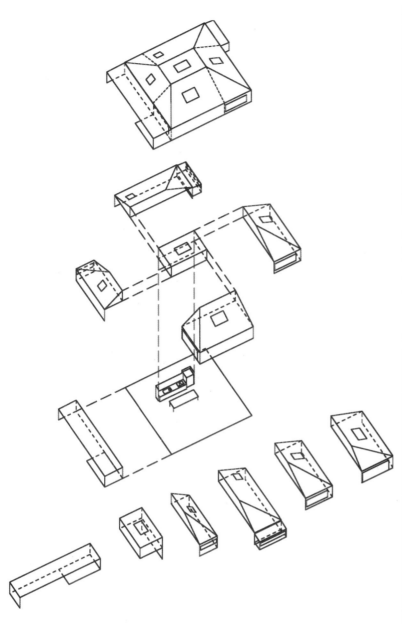

The design of the suspended walls eliminates the need for structural beams, while implying the division of the space below into "rooms".

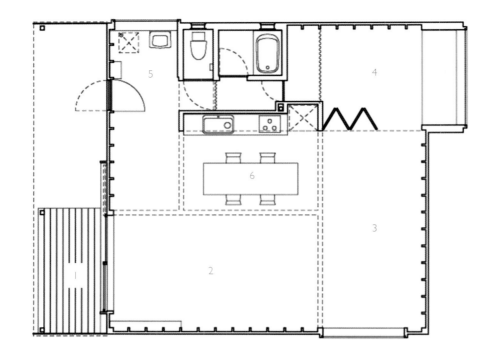

Ground floor plan

1. Terrace
2. Living room
3. Study
4. Bedroom
5. Lavatory
6. Dining room

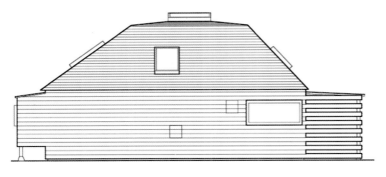

North elevation

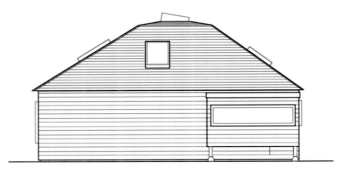

East elevation

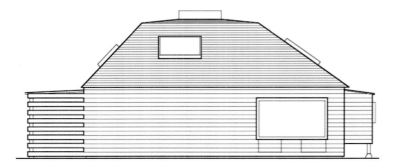

South elevation

West elevation

Section AA

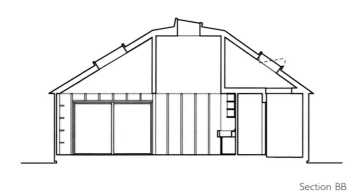

Section BB

The roof has been broken up into five planes, each facing in a different direction and each punctuated by a skylight. These skylights, along with the ample openings on each façade, ensure that the interior enjoys abundant changing light throughout the day.

A. Living room
B. Dining / Kitchen
C. Dressing room
D. Bathroom
E. Loft

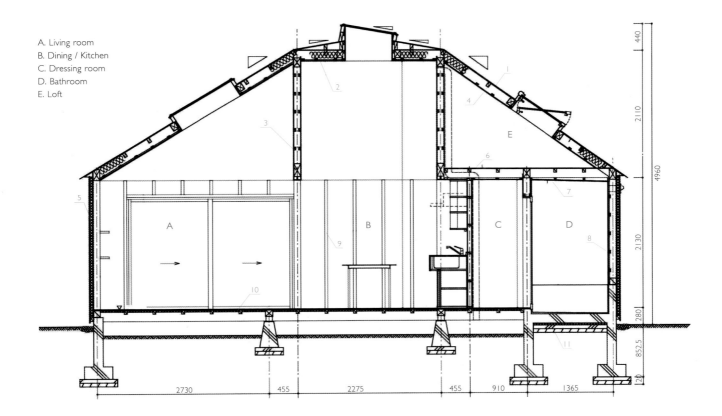

1. Galvanized and aluminum coated steel sheet, t=0.4; asphalt roofing; structural plywood, t=9
2. Plasterboard t=9.5 AEP; ceiling joist; glass wool
3. Structural plywood, t=9 AEP; furring strip
4. Lauan plywood; ceiling joist; glass wool
5. Cedar t=12; asphalt roofing; furring strip; glass wool
6. Structural plywood; floor joist

7. Flexible board t=6 AEP; furring strip
8. Flexible board t=6 AEP; lauan plywood; waterproofing sheet; furring strip
9. Stud: Western hemlock
10. Lauan plywood; structural plywood; styrofoam; floor joist
11. Styrofoam, vaporproof sheet; concrete sub-slab; crushed stone

Filippo Bombace

MB House

Rome, Italy

Photographs: Luigi Filetici

This small attic dating from the 1960s and located in a stately, yet small, Roman palace was designed by a young entrepreneur.

The mobile partitions of cellulose fiber (by Woodnotes) break the space up in a fluid and continuous progression. The space is laid out following an already consolidated network, where the primary decorative elements (the wardrobe, a bench in the sitting room the kitchen/dining room block) set the tone in this intimate ambience with its intentionally exaggerated dimensions. The palette of materials features varying tones of brown, beige, white and turquoise, as in other projects by this architect. Thus, we find the brown of the oil-treated Wengué parquet, tufa wall cladding finished in white stucco and translucent glass that brings natural light into the home.

A long, dark oak cabinet with woven linen front pieces by Elitis covering the hi-fi equipment and TV screen has been incorporated into the wall structure, which has been executed using traditional craftsmen's methods.

The living room flows directly into the dining room, which in turn extends into the kitchen.

A sliding panel provides access to the study, which doubles as a guestroom, and to the master bedroom and a bathroom.

The living room, furnished with a sofa by Mussi and "Monaco" easy chairs by Pierantonio Bonacina, is set just to the left of the entrance, which is partially concealed behind a hanging closet.

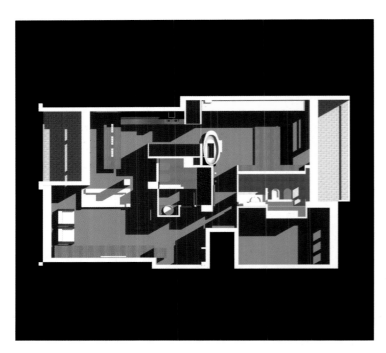

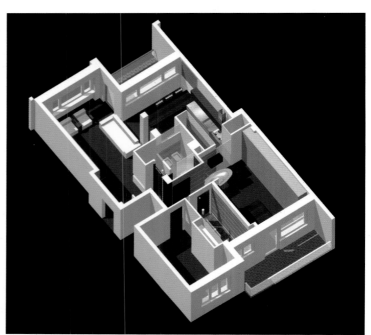

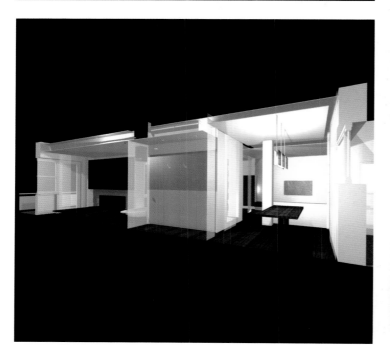

Norisada Maeda

Borzoi House

Katsuura Chiba, Japan

Photographs: Hiroshi Shinozawa

The highly experimental design for this house arose from two very specific requirements from the client. On one hand, she stipulated that the home should provide a sense of security, a feeling of looking inward; and on the other, she wanted to ensure that her pet dog, a borzoi, could not get out easily. Added to this was the architect's own passion for surfing, which he translated into the very layout in the form of a breaking wave.

"All is one inside a curving wave. Just as all the air for the living space within this giant metal curve is one," says Maeda. Thus, the floor plan for this single-story home is simple, punctuated only by three voids which bring ample light into the home and which have been filled with abundant vegetation, thereby avoiding a sense of confinement.

So, while Borzoi is "one air", there are paradoxes arrayed therein so that multiple sceneries unfurl simultaneously. The three gardens provide the necessary counterpoint to the spatial continuum of floor, walls and ceiling all being formed by the same curving surface. While the external view is a unified whole, the internal space displays obvious contours.

The structure is timber frame and steel, with the exterior completely sheathed in metal. Upon entering, though, the hard industrial feel instantly becomes gentle and welcoming, with the interior clad almost entirely in white gypsum plaster board.

The structure is timber frame and steel, with the exterior completely sheathed in metal. Upon entering, though, the hard industrial feel instantly becomes gentle and welcoming, with the interior clad almost entirely in white gypsum plaster board.

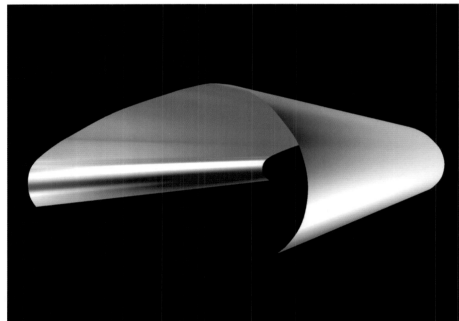

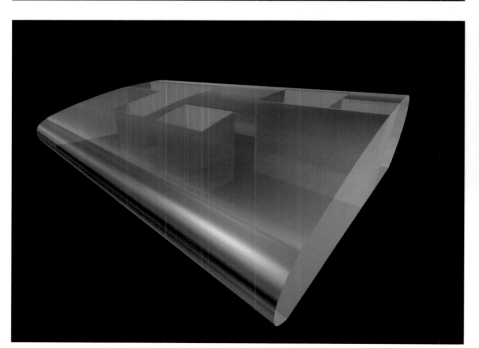

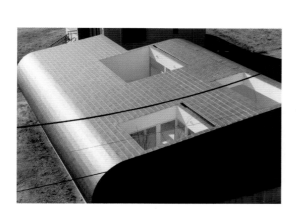

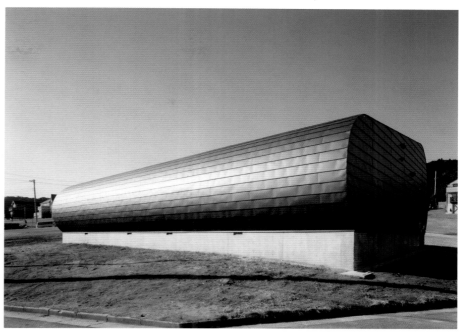

One of the guiding themes behind the design of this house was that the client's Borzoi dog should not be able to easily get out and that it should therefore have ample indoor space for exercise. The architect's response was a "runway" set along the full length of one side of the house.

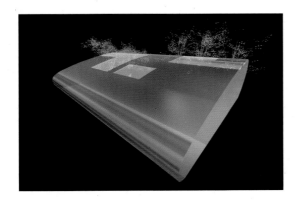

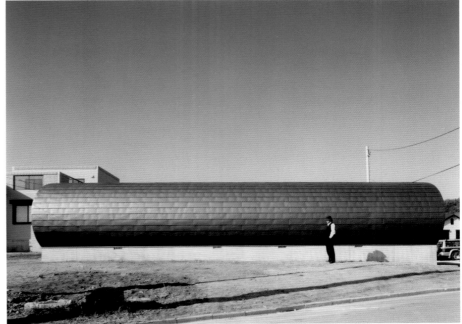

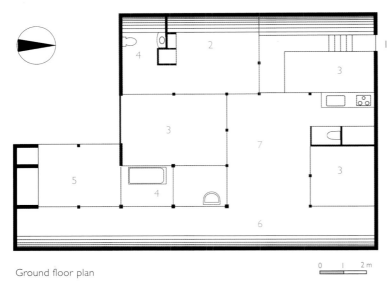

Ground floor plan

1. Entry
2. Bedroom
3. Garden
4. Bathroom
5. Tatami room
6. Dog run
7. Lounge

0   1   2 m

The structure is timber frame and steel, with the exterior completely sheathed in metal. Upon entering, though, the hard industrial feel instantly becomes gentle and welcoming, with the interior clad almost entirely in white gypsum plaster board.

Roof floor plan

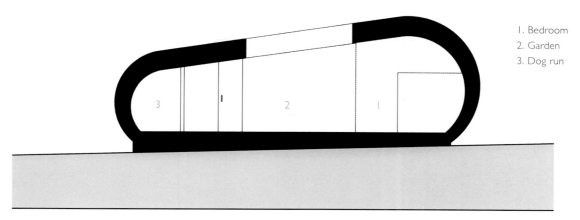

1. Bedroom
2. Garden
3. Dog run

Cross section

0   1   2 m

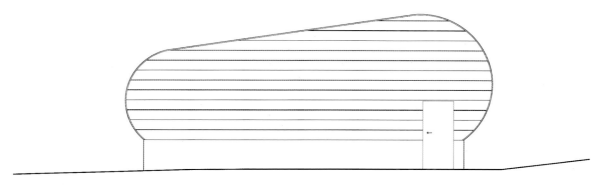

North elevation

Marcio Kogan

Br House

Rio de Janeiro, Brasil

Photographs: Nelson Kon

This 740-square-meter glass box sits on a pristine forested site in a mountainous region near Rio de Janeiro. The central design theme behind the project was to open the home out to views of the exterior as much as possible. It is almost entirely glazed, making many portions completely transparent from one side to the other. This transparency can be varied according to the placement of the movable wooden slats cladding the upper floor. In total, there are twenty meters of exterior door space, all of which can be completely opened outward, further blurring the distinction between interior and exterior. Downstairs, a massive rock has been incorporated into the structure alongside an indoor lap pool and sauna.

The home's marked horizontality is counterpoised by the wood-clad stilts on which it sits. These stilts, along with the vertical slats that adorn the upper floor, visually lift the structure upward, like the hundreds of trees surrounding it.

Guests arriving at the home leave their cars near the road and cross a steel bridge leading through the woods before reaching a tree-lined wooden deck. From here, the living room is completely exposed to outside views as the entirely glazed façade is frameless and sits flush with the floor and ceiling.

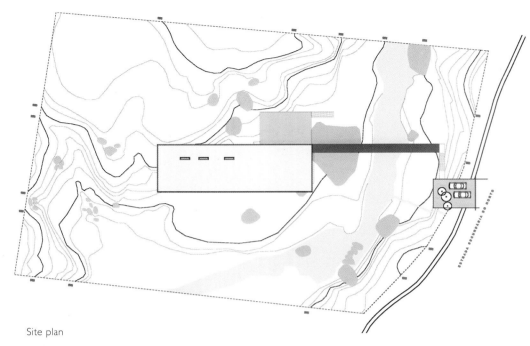

The transparency of the home can be varied according to the placement of the movable wooden slats cladding the upper floor. In total, there are twenty meters of exterior door space, all of which can be completely opened outward, further blurring the distinction between interior and exterior.

Site plan

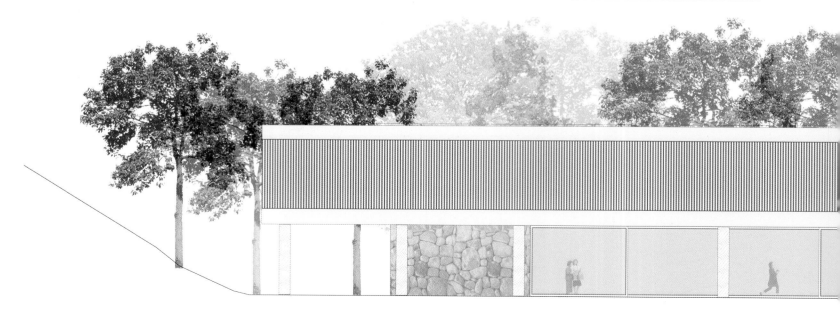

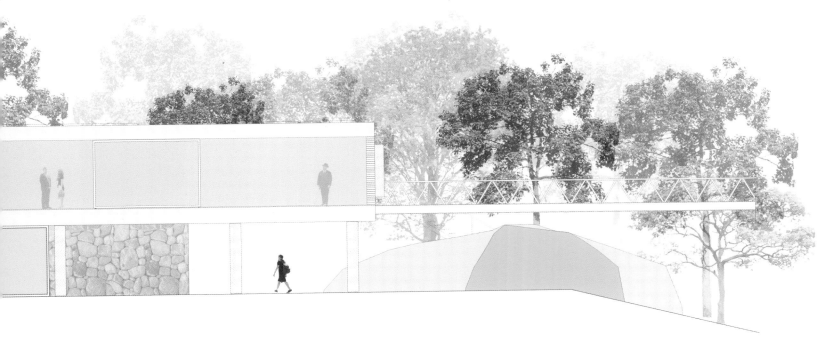

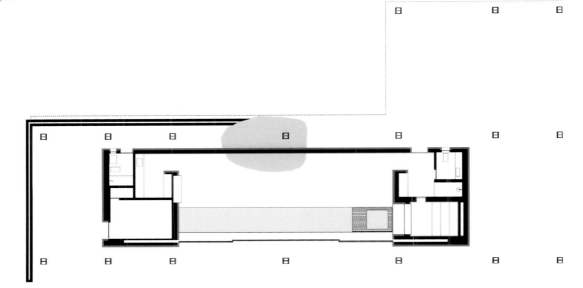

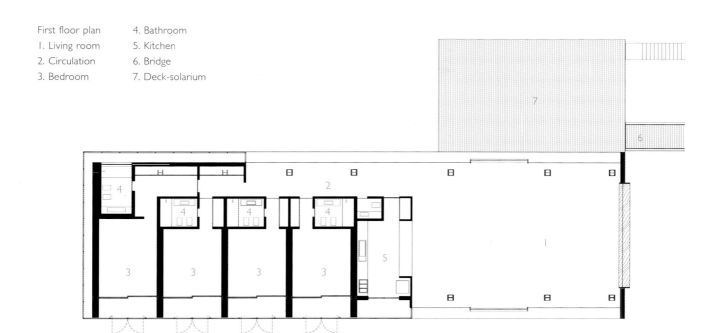

First floor plan
1. Living room   4. Bathroom
2. Circulation   5. Kitchen
3. Bedroom   6. Bridge
                7. Deck-solarium

With a façade of frameless glass inlaid into the floor and ceiling, the living room is completely exposed to views from the exterior wooden deck.

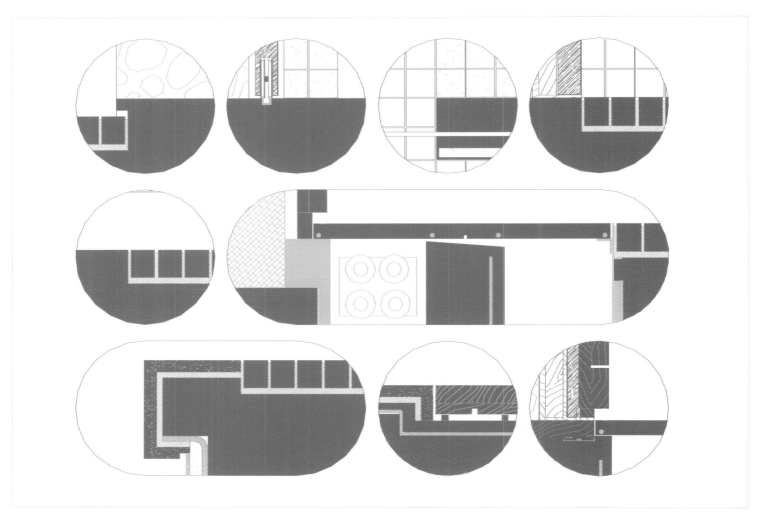

Details of joinery and other timber elements used in the house.

Dean/Wolf Architects

SoHo Skyline Loft

New York City, USA

Photographs: Jeff Goldberg / ESTO

The Soho Skyline Loft was designed in response to the surrounding skyline.

Pushing the extreme linearity of the existing conditions expanded the apartment "stage" or public room out into the visual space of the city. Here, shadows and reflections assume as much importance as built interventions.

The opposition between the windows and reflective glass walls turns a procession through the space into a passage between two skylines - one real, the other virtual and ephemeral.

At the same time, tactile cabinetry retracts away from this stage, holding the private spaces of children's bunk beds, master bedroom table and study desk.

A line of light penetrates these deep recesses, capturing morning light and creating an intimate link between the inhabitants.

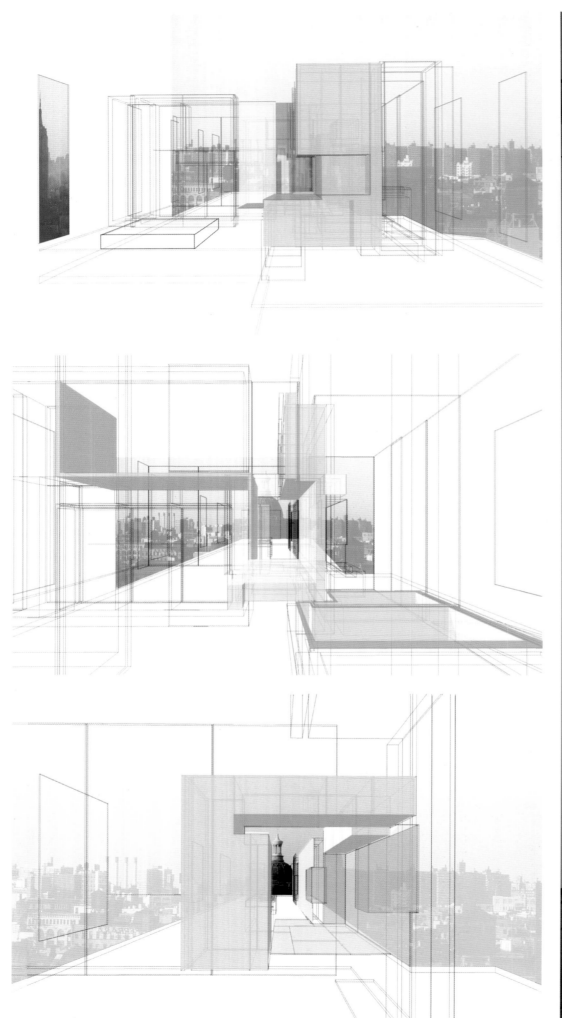

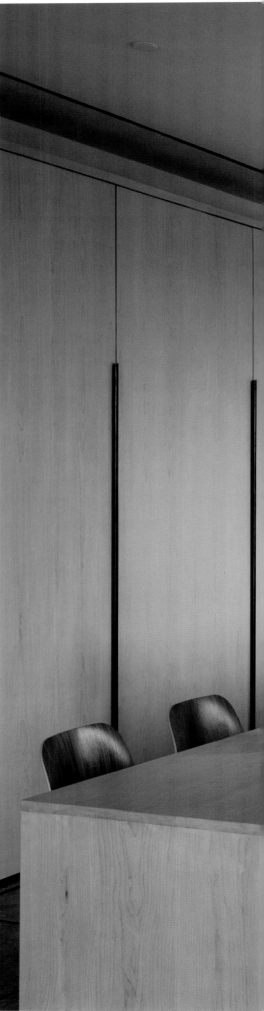

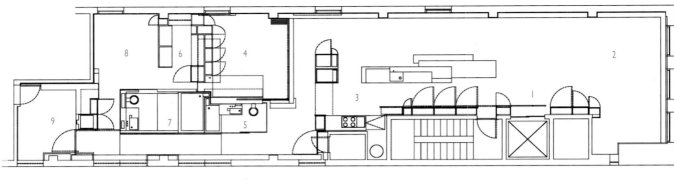

1. Entry
2. Living room
3. Kitchen
4. Bedroom
5. Bath
6. Closet
7. Master bath
8. Master bedroom
9. Office

0 1   5 m

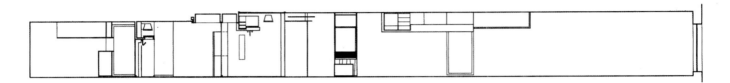

Longitudinal section

Pushing the extreme linearity of the existing conditions expanded the apartment "stage" or public room out into the visual space of the city. Here, shadows and reflections assume as much importance as built interventions.

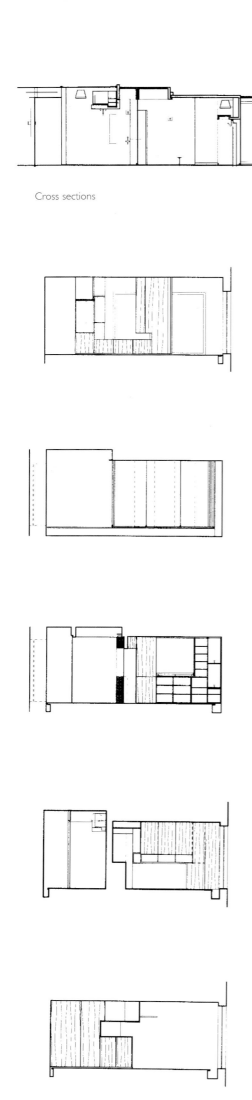

Cross sections

John Pawson

Walsh House

Telluride, California, USA

Photographs: Undine Pröhl

Central to the design of this house in the ski resort town of Telluride is its context of powerfully direct vernacular building forms. From the outside, the scale of the house is deceptively modest. With windows only on one of the side walls on the ground floor, the capacious interior volume of the second floor can hardly be guessed at. Once inside, the especially elongated single space of the upper floor is revealed and accentuated by placing the windows at both of the gable ends of the volume.

The public rooms (kitchen and living room) are on the upper floor, to take advantage of the mountain views through glazed gable ends, while bedrooms and bathrooms are on the ground floor.

By keeping to the east side of the building plot, the house maintains and enhances existing views. Likewise, each of the private rooms on the ground floor enjoys abundant natural light due to their being placed along the east wall; the long hallway and staircase are placed on the entirely closed west wall, where unwanted views of the neighboring constructions are completely blocked off.

The choice of exterior materials reflects the local palette, with quarry-cut stone flank walls, a weathered timber upper floor structure and a metal pitched roof. Inside, long straight lines and elongated forms create and heighten a sense of simplicity; the predominant materials here are stone or concrete for the floors, countertops and furnishings in wood and marble and sheets of frosted glass used as partitions.

More than any architect, Pawson has been identified with a search for simplicity, characterized as Minimalism. This design displays his trademark tendency to explore the fundamentals of space, light and materials, avoiding stylistic mannerisms.

North elevation

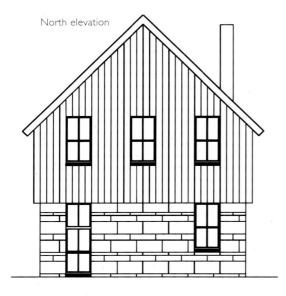

West elevation

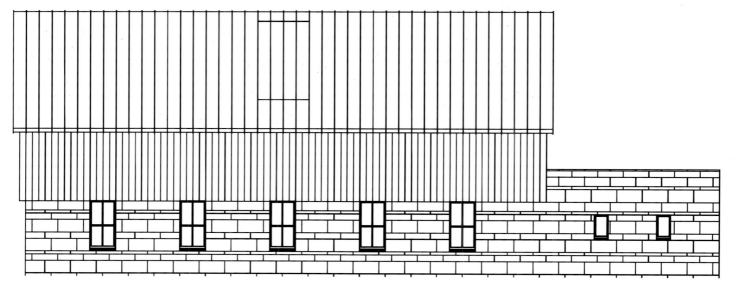

Skylights cut into the steeply pitched roof (a feature determined by local planning restrictions) bring abundant natural light into the elongated volume of the upper floor.

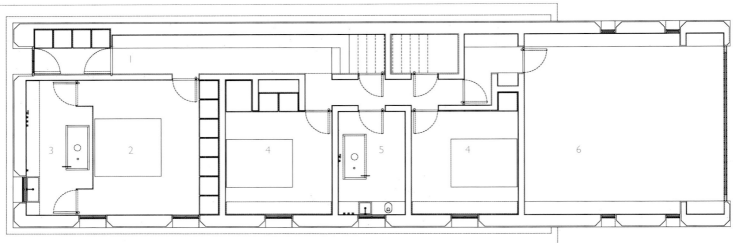

Ground floor plan

1. Entrance
2. Main bedroom
3. Main bathroom
4. Guest bedroom

5. Guest bathroom
6. Garage
7. Living area
8. Kitchen-dining
9. Terrace

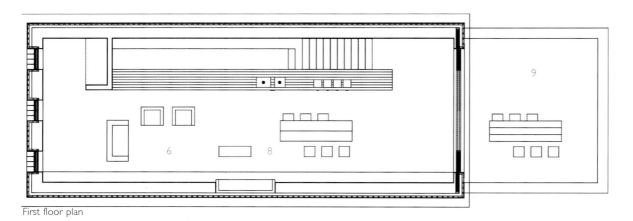

First floor plan

Light-filled slits run the length of the room above the unusually long fireplace, where roof and wall intersect, as well as below it, where the marble bench meets the wall.

On the ground floor, the private rooms are pushed against the east wall to take advantage of the site's natural light. Sheets of frosted glass have been used as partitions between the bathrooms and bedrooms, thus further enhancing the lighting scheme. The flooring throughout the house is either stone or concrete, with bathroom and kitchen fixtures done predominantly in light-hued marble.

Black Kosloff Knott Pty Ltd Architects

Wrap House

Telluride, California, USA

Photographs: John Gollings

The Wrap house is inspired by the modernist project, but rather than concentrating on the building as object, it adopts a surface-based approach. The surface of the house becomes a dynamic element that allows the manipulation of space based on light and materiality rather than form.

This design concept is expressed as a flattened plane that literally folds around the internal service blocks and 'shapes' the interior space by providing an envelope of enclosure. The service blocks, clad in metallic panels that alter color as sunlight passes through the house, serve as a counterpoint to the concrete outer shell and also demarcate the interior space.

Spatially, the house is organized so that the service areas and the internal dividing walls are centrally located, which allows the external 'skin' of the building to be experienced as an independent element. The house has an unusual layout, with different areas flowing into each other differentiated by their varying heights and volumes. This is exemplified by the fact that an observer can stand at one end of the house and see directly through to the other end across a number of varied and differentiated volumes.

The house is located on a site that rises sharply from street level and plateaus out around two meters above the footpath. The main living spaces are located on the higher level and project out onto the street, with a bedroom located above providing views over the neighboring houses to the city beyond. The house is embedded into the local fabric as a surface that rises out of the landscape, and the experience from the upper levels is one of being 'nestled' into its context, surrounded by pitched roofs.

Environmental aspects were an important part of the design, which incorporates various energy saving techniques including maximum glazing to the north, no windows in the southern wall and a large pergola shading the windows along the entire northern façade.

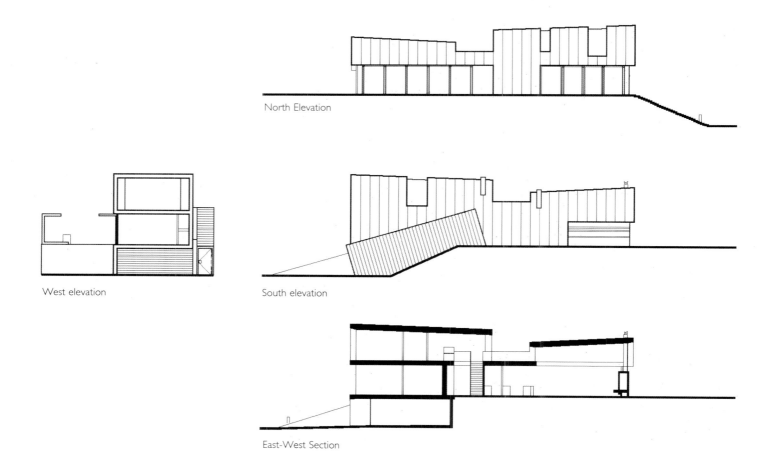

North Elevation

West elevation

South elevation

East-West Section

Entry is through a concentrated and slightly disorienting entry tube wrapped in a continuous surface which suddenly expands to a double-height, sun-filled stairwell. The progression throughout the house alternates between service areas that compress the space and large, light rooms, with the living area connecting directly to the garden.

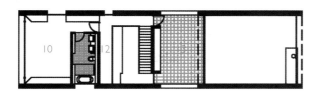

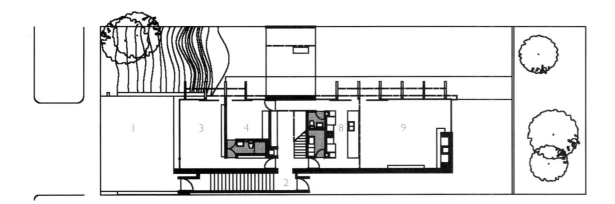

Ground floor

1. Driveway
2. Entry Stair
3. Library
4. Bedroom
5. Bathroom
6. Laundry
7. W. C
8. Kitchen
9. Living/Dining

First floor

10. Master Bedroom
11. Ensuite
12. Office
13. Roof Deck
14. Garage

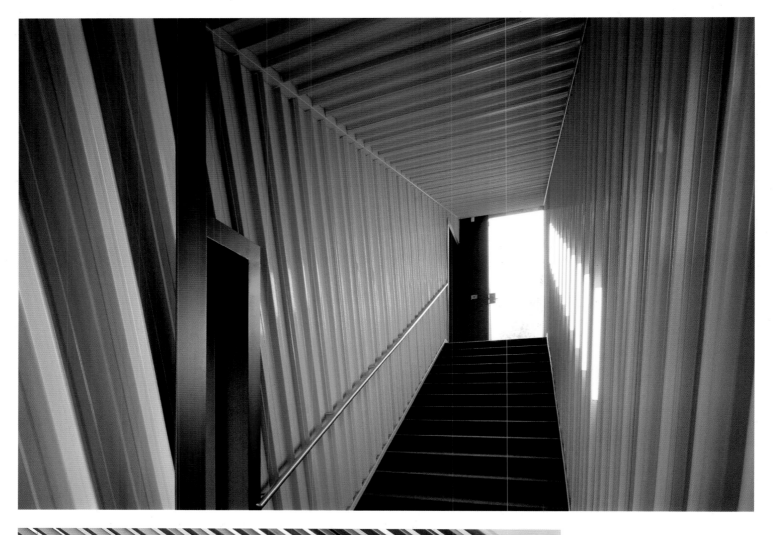

The clients, in their 60's, had significant input into the design with a highly detailed brief constantly evolving throughout this process. They wanted an flexible layout that could be reconfigured according to their changing needs.

Johanna Grawunder

Beach House in Milan

Milan, Italy

Photographs: Santi Caleca

The design approach for the interior of this beach house was to look for the "essence" of the existing open space and respect it as much as possible.

This was achieved by painting the existing concrete structure matt black in order to highlight it, so that the structure itself became the most striking element of the loft. The emphasis was on creating an easy and elegant environment, using mainly inexpensive materials, and leaving different areas as open as possible while allowing the structure to define the space.

The few volumes in the space arose from the need for some private areas within this very strong cultural grid. In order to respect the mainly post and beam construction, the few walls that where required were designed to look like separate volumes, huddling under the structural grid.

Paint was used to define the space and create different effects, black for the structural grid, light blue for the ceiling, and different shades of green and gray for the volumes. The finishes and furniture were carefully chosen to create an environment where various levels of refinement could comfortably coexist - a few custom designed pieces mixed with other simple and inexpensive or industrial-style furniture.

The house consists of a master bedroom and bathroom, a simple kitchen and an open plan living area. Sliding doors separate the bedroom from the main room, so that it can be open to the rest of the house. The emphasis is on maximum flexibility of use and movement through the space.

Interior elevation

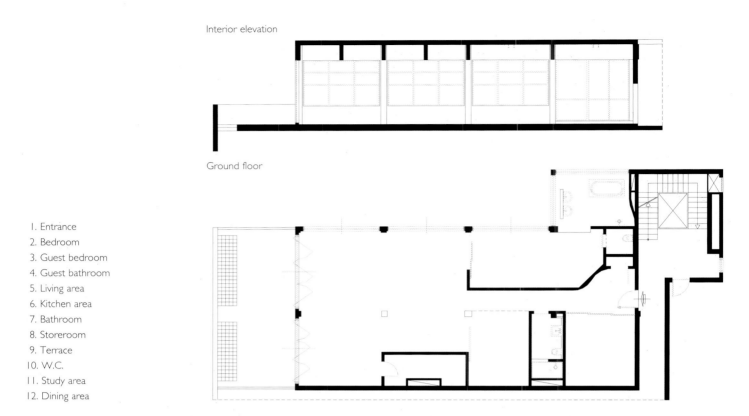

Ground floor

1. Entrance
2. Bedroom
3. Guest bedroom
4. Guest bathroom
5. Living area
6. Kitchen area
7. Bathroom
8. Storeroom
9. Terrace
10. W.C.
11. Study area
12. Dining area

The living room is the main open loft-like space and has only basic furniture, mostly out of the way, so that there is maximum flexibility. The simple black laminate kitchen opens up to the rest of the main room, with two steel carts which serve as storage and a preparation island.

Mathias Klotz

Viejo House

Santiago de Chile, Chile

Photographs: Roland Halbe / ARTUR

The Viejo house is a single family residence located in a residential neighborhood of Santiago dating from the 1950s.

An existing house on the site was demolished and replaced with a new building, which makes the best of the large trees in the garden. The house is based on a 12 x 40 m rectangle plan, placed at the back of the site in order to leave a large open area at the front. The internal layout was resolved on a single level, and the building is made entirely of reinforced concrete.

The concrete on the outside surfaces is exposed and treated with different textures in order to create contrast between the different areas. The layout is based around two corridors, one internal and the other external, that move from the entrance towards the main bedroom. The more public areas are near the entrance, with the more public spaces towards the back.

It is a peaceful building that subtly resolves the construction and layout problems using differences in the texture on the outside, and height differences on the inside areas, according to use and proportion.

The roof of the house was transformed into a terrace, using the level changes of the flagstones to advantage and creating 360 degree views of the hills surrounding the city of Santiago.

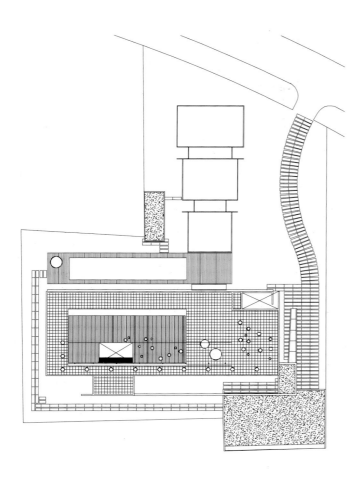

This house, located in a 1950's residential neighborhood, is based on a 12×14 m rectangular design placed at the far end of a 3,600 m² site.
Built entirely from reinforced concrete, it occupies 600 m² and takes advantage of the finest trees that were originally on the site.

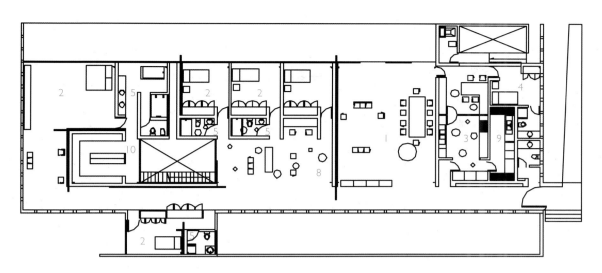

1. Living Room
2. Bedroom
3. Kitchen
4. Service room
5. Bathroom
6. Patio
7. Terrace
8. Family room - Guest room
9. Laundry room
10. Dressing room

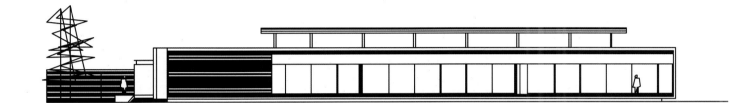

This building subtly resolves construction and layout issues by working with different textures for the exposed concrete, and using height differences on the interior spaces, according to their use and proportions.

Izquierdo + Lehmann

Vial House

Santiago de Chile, Chile

Photographs: Roland Halbe / ARTUR

This 360-square-meter house was built on a plot measuring more than 1300 m² in the privileged setting of El Mirador de San Damián. Logically, the project had to satisfy the multiple requirements arising from such relevant factors as place, with its characteristics of access, terrain, topography, orientation and views, plus the dimensions and shape of the plot; the program of usage, with various combinations of enclosures and openings; construction costs, durability and deadlines and the applicable zoning and construction laws.

Using this framework as a basis, there still remained the question of how to bring the idea of what a house is to fruition. Essentially, a home must provide a sense of intimacy. Here, this is manifested architecturally through a regulated interplay of light and shadow on the smooth, white planes of the walls and ceilings, marking the passage of time with their rhythm of days and changing seasons (as intimacy is granted parsimoniously), along with the feeling of weightlessness of the materials of which it is composed. In contrast, the concrete bulk of the exterior walls and slabs was left untreated and exposed to the view and touch.

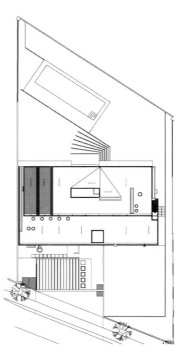

This 360-square-meter house was built on a plot measuring more than 1300 m² in the privileged setting of El Mirador de San Damián. The project seeks to optimally reconcile such conditioning factors as place, the size and shape of the plot, the program, interior-exterior relations, cost and deadlines and, of course, the applicable regulations.

Ground floor plan

First floor plan

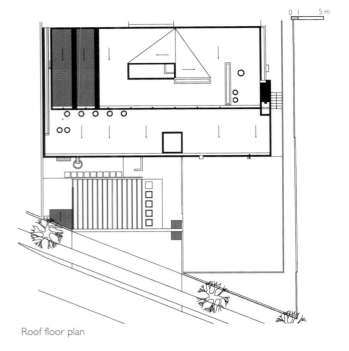

Roof floor plan

The desire to ensure privacy is manifested architecturally through an interplay of light and shadow on the smooth, white planes of the walls and ceilings, along with the feeling of weightlessness of the materials of which it is composed. In contrast, the concrete bulk of the exterior walls and slabs was left untreated and exposed to the view and touch.

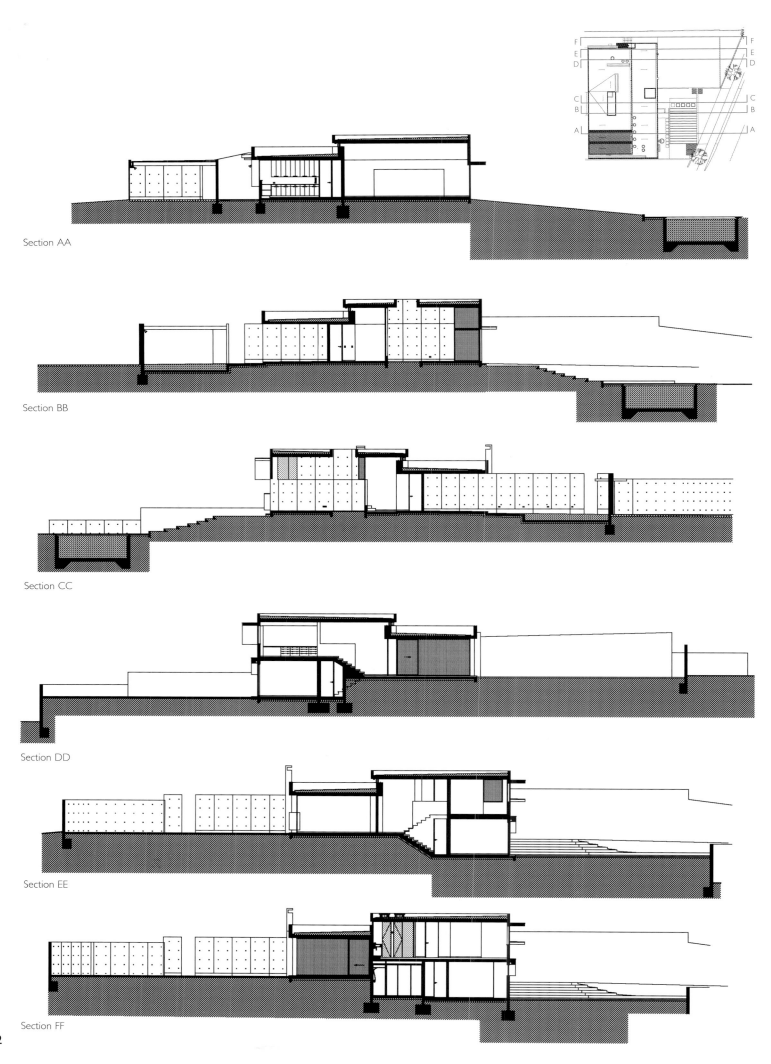

Section AA

Section BB

Section CC

Section DD

Section EE

Section FF

212

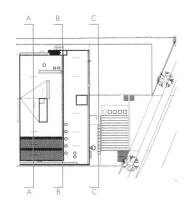

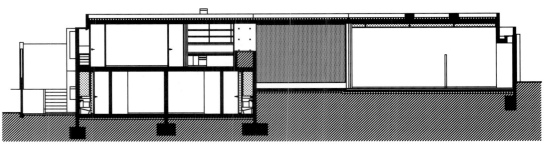

Section GG

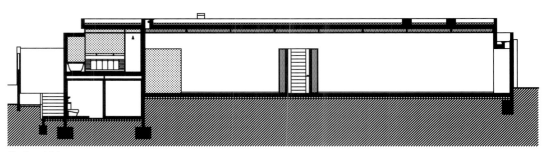

Section HH

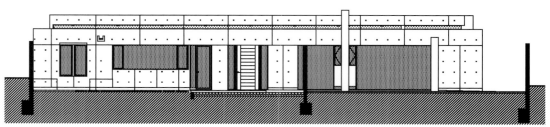

Section II

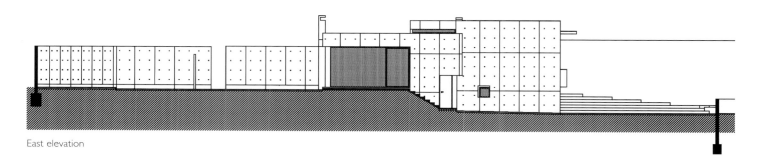

East elevation

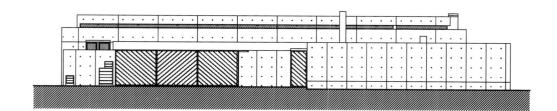

South elevation

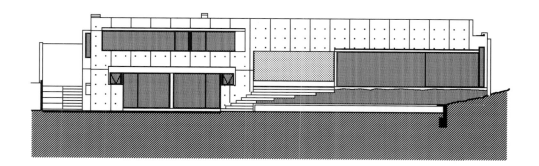

North elevation

214

Takaharu + Yui Tezuka / Tezuka Architects,
Masahiro Ikeda / mias

Engawa House

Tokyo, Japan

Photographs: Katsuhisa Kida

The Engawa House was designed to accommodate a single family. To the north of the site is the grandparents' home, with the eldest son and his family living on the second floor. The building-to-land ratio in the area is high and most houses take up the entire surface of properties, leaving no space for a garden. The grandparents' home was no exception, with its southern engawa (a multifunctional space which roughly corresponds to the veranda) facing a massive wall at a distance of only 50 centimeters. That is precisely where their daughter and her husband decided to settle when by chance the southern lot was put up for sale.

Plans were thus laid out for a long, narrow building bordering the south road. An open area along the northern side would provide space for an inner garden, which, being set alongside a low, one-story house, would receive plenty of light. The southern roadside wall was erected to a height of 2.2 meters, with a high-side opening that would protect the family's privacy while giving a clear view of the sky. On the other side, floor-to-ceiling windows provide a full perspective of the garden. The result is a 16.2-meter-long and 4.6-meter-wide space encased between two L-shaped frames.

Wood was chosen as the main construction material because it ensures a monolithic sense of unity, but the length of the openings meant that reinforcements had to be added. The difference in height of the northern and southern openings gives the whole structure an unusual appearance, like uneven parallel bars. Visual lines are interrupted, but the space itself was conceived as one single volume.

Nine sliding doors allow the house to open completely on the garden side. And so when a group of family and friends gathered at a garden party to celebrate the completion of the building, the idea naturally arose that the whole structure resembled an engawa.

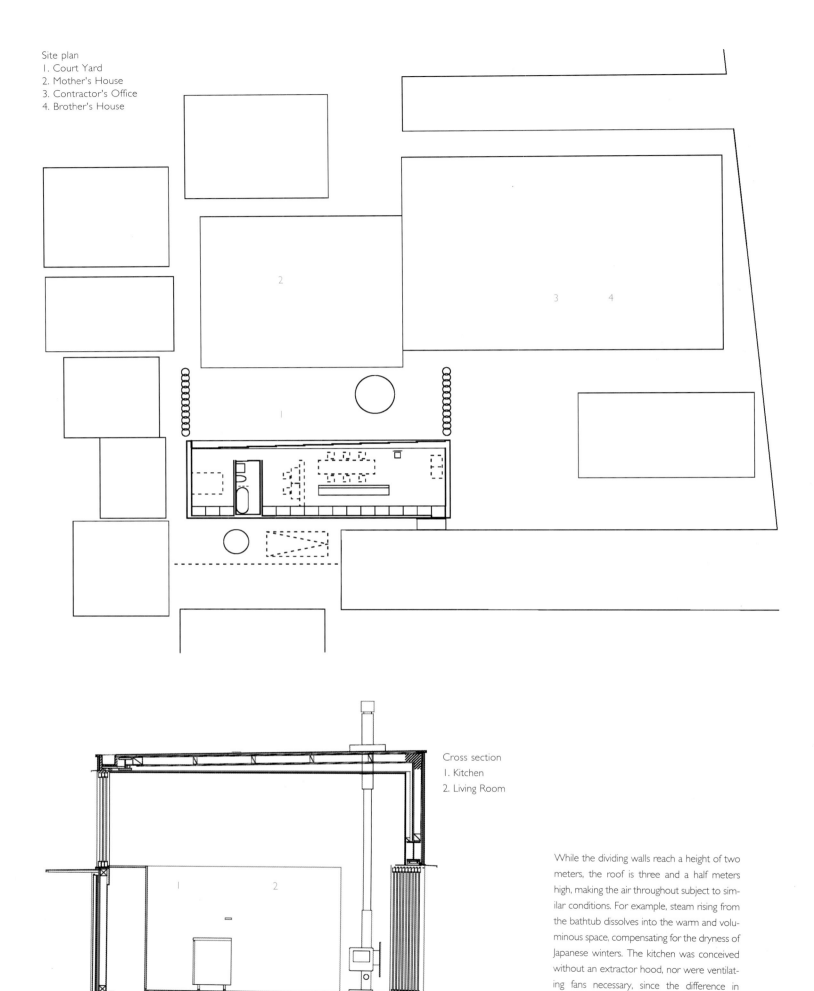

Site plan
1. Court Yard
2. Mother's House
3. Contractor's Office
4. Brother's House

Cross section
1. Kitchen
2. Living Room

While the dividing walls reach a height of two meters, the roof is three and a half meters high, making the air throughout subject to similar conditions. For example, steam rising from the bathtub dissolves into the warm and voluminous space, compensating for the dryness of Japanese winters. The kitchen was conceived without an extractor hood, nor were ventilating fans necessary, since the difference in height of the northern and southern openings creates a natural airflow. In the summer, hot air rises toward the roof and naturally exits through the high-side opening.

218

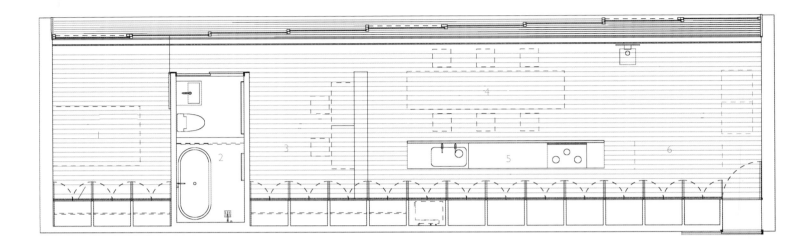

Floor plan
1. Master Bedroom
2. Bathroom
3. Children's Room
4. Dining Room
5. Kitchen
6. Living Room

Uras + Dilekci Architects

Misir loft

Istanbul, Turkey

Photographs: Ali Bekman

The Misir building, designed by Armenian architect Hovsep Aznavour in 1910, is located in the central Beyoglu district of Istanbul. The brief por this project was to create a 280 m² loft on the second floor of this building to serve as a second city home for a couple who enjoy entertaining. With this in mind, the architects focussed on retaining some of the original character of the space, while transforming it into a highly original, modern and flexible apartment.

Near the entrance and in the kitchen, the floor was lifted to create a counters which can be used for dining and working. Changing color strips of light were embedded in the floor below, and can be programmed to create different moods. The lighting in most of the house, including a custom made chandelier, is made from simple black electrical wire and hanging lightbulbs, and strategically placed mirrored surfaces create different effects. The original brick and structural timber was exposed in places in order to keep the original flavor of the building, and the plaster ceilings were burnt with a torch to create an organic texture.

In the bedroom, which can be completely closed off from the rest of the apartment by a 360 degree black velvet curtain, one of the walls is made of glass and the other is a remote controlled, red PVC lacquared door.

In the bathroom, oval marble and steel pieces were cut out and placed into the screed to create a terrazzo-like textured floor, and the cabinets were custom made using bamboo verneer.

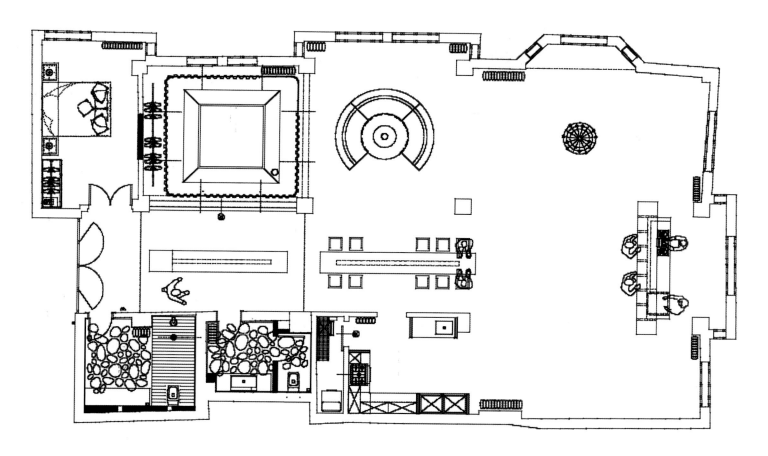

This apartment was conceived as a second residence for entertaining and leisure. The open spaces, furniture, lighting and construction design reflect this unusual brief.

The bedroom is the only "closed" space in the apartment, and can be isolated from the rest of the space using black velvet curtains. A green circular dining booth was designed by Atelier Derin to serve more formal dinners in the space, and a screen which slides down over the glass wall separating the bedroom and the dining area can be used for screening films.

Claesson Koivisto Rune

No.5 House

Nacka, Sweden

Photographs: Åke E:son Lindman

The starting point for this house for a graphic designer and his family (the client designed the No. 5 sign himself) was a simple structure where the inside would be as important as the outside. The design was developed as a geometric volume, a kind of inverted volume that can be read either as a box with a series of openings, or an open space with a series of closures. The construction method involved establishing a grid based on standard dimensions for building materials, and then superimposing it onto the basic box structure. This grid was used to create the basic room structure for the house, which included three bedrooms, a bathroom and one larger living/dining space with kitchen. One of the four sides of each of the main rooms was completely glazed, allowing natural light into the house and blurring the distinction between interior and exterior. The bedrooms and living area are basically open towards one cardinal point each, meaning there is an opening in each facade. Even though the bedrooms are quite small, the surrounding landscape becomes part of the space, creating a sense of vastness. The bathroom, which has no wall opening, has a roof window instead. A glazed doorway leading out from the living area to a partially walled terrace creates an outdoor room that is open to the sky at one end and open to the view at the other.

The design for this house is based on a geometric volume in which the interior and the exterior are equally important. One of the walls of each room is totally glazed, so that the landscape becomes part of the interior and makes it appear larger. The house has a terrace that is partially enclosed, open to the sky on one side and the views on the other.

Site plan

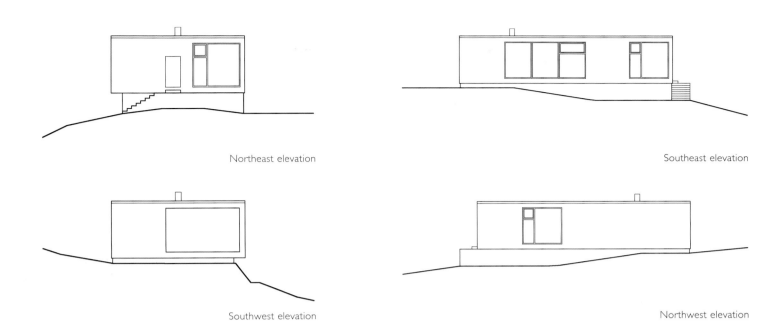

Northeast elevation

Southeast elevation

Southwest elevation

Northwest elevation

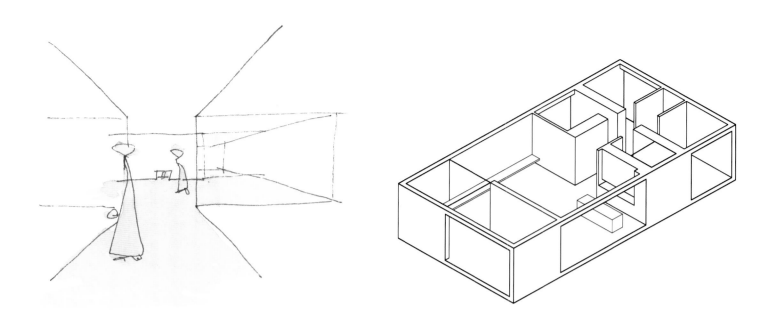

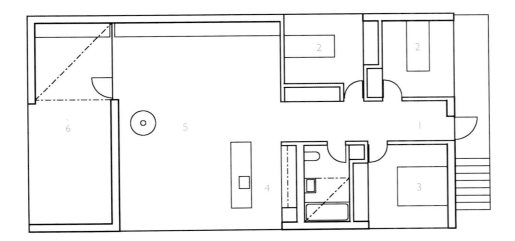

1. Entrance
2. Bedroom
3. Master bedroom
4. Kitchen
5. Living
6. Terrace

010846133